BrandinG

Logos & Marks / Elements of Branding Design

LOGOS & MARKS

ICO

A picture is a fact.

- Ludwig Wittgensten

Mike Quon Designation Inc
Mike Quon
543 River Road, Fair Haven, New Jersey 07704
United States

'Simplicity is the ultimate sophistication'.

- Leonardo DaVinci

Logos, trademarks, symbols, corporate identity, branding, image, packaging, wordmarks, and on and on.

It is a visual world, and the idea of visually trademarking ones business and services is a valuable concept. In the world of marketing, it is simply a requirement to compete effectively. Business people worldwide embrace this idea. Logos, icons, and wordmarks overwhelm the visual landscape. Today they seem to appeal on a more personal and friendly level. Characters of all kinds; abstract symbols, monograms, and more are out there competing for our attention and business dollars. Whatever the product or service, it is about defining and communicating a clear and simple message: quality, stability, and individuality. These logos, logotypes, and brandmarks are promoted and advertised continuously to embed in the consumerÉÜs mind their message of improved lifestyle, reliable service, and more.

As designers, our job is to find out what the clientÉÜs needs and goals are and what their message is. Then we create visual shortcuts to convey a positive and attractive ÉÑtone and mannerÉÜ that will clearly relay the clientÉÜs message to the consumer. Whatever the identity, it must also work on all printed matter, including business cards, signage, websites, print advertising media, television, etc. And hopefully this brand will stand out on the world stage and be recognizable, familiar, and in style. Besides creating an image that the client falls in love with, the identity has work to do in the world of marketing to generate increased sales and repeat customers.

A lot of money and time are spent on the perception generated by a brand image and to create an interest in it. Through design, we are underscoring the feeling and perception that a consumer trusts the brand we identify. Logos, taglines, names, packaging, sophisticated advertising, photography, and illustration all contribute to this. The most successful brand identities take simple design elements and use them repeatedly to reinforce the product image and message. NikeÉÜs is among the most famous,with its swoosh logo. And Starbucks, with its warm, comfortable and trend-setting style, uses all of its visual space to encourage people to buy their coffee. Their logo,

packaging, signage, and interiors all work together to evoke the feeling that their product is desirable.

Clients realize that designers can have a major impact on their sales and marketing, and can spend a lot of money in this pursuit. Design has a big role in the sales campaign. For example, products such as perfume and soda rely heavily on image and packaging since so many of these products are essentially the same. Take the Gap for example. There are many clothing companies that have similar quality and style, but donÉÜt have nearly the outreach and loyal audience. Advertising and brand image is hugely responsible for this. The Gap's simple and bold logo, and its marketing campaign evoking a happy, carefree lifestyle seem to be paying big dividends on the bottom line each year.

Getting the viewers attention is important, but in the end the product or service must be able to keep the customer on a long term basis as repeat business is critical to success. The product has to stand behind its advertising to truly be successful, as many companies have spent large sums of money on building their brands and have seen a short-term gain or no gain at all. In other words, the customer wants the goods and services delivered as promised. Fedex with its tagline 'the world on time' positions itself effectively and really delivers, in more ways than one.

As Leonardo DaVinci said, 'simplicity is the ultimate sophistication'. For marketing, few do it better than Nike. And for profitably: ideally, getting your message across in a simple mark, logotype, or symbol in todayÉÜs overcrowded marketplace will positively impact the bottom line. Keeping it simple, a brand identity can communicate effectively to people of all ages around the globe, inspiring confidence and enthusiasm.

Designers should also remember that while we are being creative, we are also in the business of building brands. Our job is to understand the problem, find a solution, and make the identity stand out in our visually over-saturated world. Brand identities are indispensable to marketing a product, and the best-designed and most successful identities are often the most valuable asset a company can have.

Mike Quon / Mike Quon Designation Inc.

Art Associates Amsterdam
Eddie Archer
W.G. Plein 378
1054 SG Amsterdam

tel: +31 20 6830535
fax +31 20 6121517
info@artassociates.nl
http://www.artassociates.nl

What precisely is a logo?

A logo is a symbol, a shape and or a word, it can be shaped, designed, or in the case of a word, consist of specially designed lettering.

It's a way for a company or business to show its own unique 'face' and a way to communicate the core spirit of one's company to the world.

No business can do without it in this day and age.

Each and every logo has its own unique way of communicating a certain 'show and value' (vision and mission). One feels either safe or modern, relaxed or exited, depending on what the logo expresses in feeling.

A good logo is a good design and the designing of a logo is a great creative process, as it expresses the company's identity and strategy. It will not need any further explanation or embellishment.

Large or small, a good logo is effective and clear and always reflects the quality of the company, whatever the circumstances. For example: even if it's a full colour design, it always also works effectively in black and white.

A logo, if it is well designed, is a symbol that is totally practical in all its uses. It's a marvelous thing and something to be admired and used as a priceless communicative tool.

Some examples of instantly recognizable logo's: Shell, Philips,Toyota, Esso, Coca Cola, Mercedes Benz, Disney, MacDonald's, Apple, Sony..

A pictogram.

What is a pictogram?

The exact meaning of the word pictogram is a simple image or instruction.

It points to a function or a location, a warning or instruction on how to use something. A good example of this usage would be traffic signs. Or the signage used in places like airports, where it's important that the signs are internationally understandable in a compact, visual form, known as an icon.

The meaning of this 'picto' should be instantly recognisable, thereby eradicating the need to use text or words to give an instruction.

It is essential that in a busy area, such as a railway station this information has a very clear form and attracts one's attention in such a way that it makes text unnecessary.

Pictos have been used for hundreds of years; think of for example the signs outside shops or inns, or gable stones on houses. The use of pictos as a sort of international language can have very effective cost advantages by allowing each land to use the same symbols.

Pictos must be simple, easy to recognize, easy to learn and remember. They also must take up less space than text and be instantly identifiable. Their function becomes a language in itself. In our modern high velocity world of communication and globalization these kinds of images have become increasingly indispensable. Consumers need instant information.

The use of pictos in such things as LED displays in automobiles and hi-tech machines and computers and other modern apparatus is increasing daily, which would indicate that we will be needing, using and therefore creating more of these type of images in the future. Also by not taking so much space as textand by being instantly identifiable the function of pictos becomes a language in itself.

Eddie Archer / Art Associates Amsterdam

Russell Leong Design
Russell K. Leong
847 Emerson Street Palo Alto,
California 94301
United States

Is the logo really dead?

Many years ago, I read in a design publication that a very promi-
nent graphic designer specializing in corporate branding
declared that the logo was dead.
Even at the time, I thought to myself, that can he possibly mean
by that?
Are the there too many logos in existence?
Are they no longer necessary?
Have they lost their effectiveness?
Who killed them?
I've pondered that statement for many years since then.
However, to this day, I am still convinced that the statement is
true in many ways, but is also false in others.

The logo can never die, it human nature that if one has a product
or service to promote, one is inclined to personalize or brand it in
some way or another to differentiate it from others.
To do it in a way that is creative and memorable is characteristic
of individuals who are creating innovative goods and services.

Perhaps the logo lost its effectiveness because there were too
many good logos produced and that for one to stand out among
them was no longer possible.
Too much of a good thing? In a perfect world of nothing but well
designed logotypes and marks, maybe there a place for poorly
designed, ugly, or strangely unique ones to stand out or even
shine. Perhaps that is yet another story.

On the other hand, Apple Computer revealed its ground-break-
ing logo in the early eighties with a less than normal graphic of a
multi-colored striated apple.
A stylized apple as a corporate mark for an innovative computer
company?
It was radical departure from the accepted corporate look that
had been in place in the technology world for many years.

Apple had almost single-handedly changed the dynamic of how
corporate brand identity was done in the Silicon Valley (high-
technology sector) with its bold commitment in design.

In a more recent development, the internet has spawned an ugly
mutation in the corporate logotype world.

You can now actually have a logo developed by a internet-based
entity for as low as $29.99 each.
What you get for that price is questionable and not particularly
well designed, but has, nevertheless, been designed by a design
professional (loosely termed as a person who designs for a living).

My point is that there will always be new and revolutionary logos
developed but they will always exist within a world of less than
interesting and poorly designed logos.
At least that what I hoping for.

That what makes life interesting from a logotype developer per-
spective.
Without all the ineffective logos in the world, we cannot fully
appreciate the well designed and innovative logos that are produced.

Russell K. Leong
Russell Leong Design

Guerrini Design Island
Sebastian Guerrini
Paraguay 754 4B, Buenos
Aires (CP 1057),
Argentina

Branding issues

Branding is important for the current social life, for business, for collective identities and for man's soul, allowing people to identify, organise, classify, embody and get sense of the world.

Issues on branding are issues about identity or, more precisely, about identification, which can be understood, in a psychoanalytical sense, as the transformation that takes place when someone or something assumes an image. The identifying process with images is dynamic, because it is always bridging social images to personal ones, the entity taking just some of them as proper, and rejecting the rest of the existing images. This selection is constantly questioning or reinforcing the way the observers see their own identity by forcing the beholders to explain themselves in their positions, in their differential belonging to other images considered to be themselves, to other conclusions, other stories, discourses and collective identifications. It is within this struggle among images - and as Foucault states it - that the image's Design becomes powerful when entering the domain of other discourses.

One could ask why this power works, and an anthropological answer would be that nothing socially exists until it is being represented. In that way, representation might well be part of the resources that make any social bond alive, making visible and tangible any membership or relationship. On the other hand, people, organisations, companies or objects need image to perform the dynamic process of leading their closure of structuring totalities in order to have their individualisation.

But if identification is related to images...what is an image? An image is an intentional cut-out of the world surrounding us, which reaches the status of an entity in itself. That entity, that image, can be powerful in imposing meaning and sense in a sudden way to those who see it, and this is achieved by means of two

qualities of visual media. First, its parts act as words that articulate representations like information in the way of a text. Second, the strength arisen by the construction of that instantaneous, synthetic, organic and organised discursive whole confuses the perceptions in the spectator, naturalising or presenting an assembly of fragments as some meaningful real.

Thus, identification can be understood as the embodiment with images of object discourses, something proper of the corporate branding, and the visual embodiment of ideological discourses, something proper of the institutional or political branding. Besides, both are part of human resources to structure and give sense to all components of reality, which is something proper of branding.

Sebastian Guerrini
Guerrini Design Island

Lumen Srl.
Drew Smith
Via Tortona, 4 - 20144 Milan,
Italy

How well we apply our creativity to understanding, interpreting and expressing a brand's identity directly affects its value in the market.

A brand is the most valuable asset of a company. It's an agreement with a consumer to satisfy their expectations. How well we can help our clients understand and develop this relationship is fundamental to a brand's long term success.

Design consultancies have a key role to play in helping clients think "outside the box", applying creativity to the development of innovative brand strategies.

In the past this role has been filled by advertising agencies. Unfortunately, ad agencies by their very nature are short-term oriented, interested in applying strategy to sell campaigns, not to build up long term brand equity for clients.

There is a great deal of confusion surrounding what brand identity consultancies actually do. We do not create identities. We create brands and images that express identities and create long term relationships with customers. Quite often this image is the only thing that gives added value to a company's product or service.
We are at the service of marketing and marketing exists for one reason only:

To create a difference.

I'm surprised, and disappointed, when I get briefs that only talk about USP's.
Unique selling propositions, they rarely exist anymore.
Or if they do, they don't last very long before being copied by the competition.
A great mistake that is often made by marketing is to link the identity of a brand to the performance of a product or service.

More often than not it's the brand itself, not the product that makes the difference.

A brand's appeal and value lies in its capacity to reinvent itself. This innovation must be based on the values of that brand, both real and perceived. It is important to understand the perception of that brand in the eyes of the consumer.

Branding is at the same time complex and extremely simple. A complex process that begins with a very simple question. Why does this brand exist?

It's a question that a lot of marketing managers would have trouble answering, but this raison d'etre becomes a critical issue in todays competitive markets. It's the first step in understanding the identity behind the brand. Its the thing that gives meaning to a brand and an advantage over the competition.

Many brands exist today solely because they've always existed. Few brands really know who they are, what they believe in and what makes them unique.

Drew Smith Lumen /
Italy

Scribblers' Club
Eric Sweet
969 Guelph Street, Kitchener,
Ontario, Canada

You're not really going to wear that are you?

It's easily one of the most erroneously and overused "ABC Company Inc." boardroom phrases of the day. First on the agenda "We are losing market share, we need to re-brand the company, what we need is a new logo..." this vocalized spark of brilliance is followed lemur-like by a line of resonating bobble heads parked in high back leather chairs surrounding the battleship of a table. Interesting.

Those same executives started with that same ABC Co. some time ago and all of them joined with a predisposition of what it was that ABC Co. was all about. Who was ABC Co, what did it do, how did it do it, for what gains and at what costs, and for whom? At one end of the table you have corporate efficacy, the side of the corporations brain that needs to generate profits for it's stakeholders, while the other side of the corporate brain is dealing with the consumer. What is forgotten is the connection between each side of the equation. One of the issues facing many traditional company's decision makers is their distance from the front lines of their company. Burdened with diluted field research and stacks of data they have lost sight of the bigger picture, ABC Co. consumers. Not all companies behave this way, in fact some of the most successful are ones that stay very attuned to their end users. Sounds simple enough.

Brand is more than a logo mark and phrasing. Brand is all that the company wears when it greets its suppliers and clients each and every day for each and every interaction. The company brand is the cumulative emotive response to every touchpoint the world has with the company. From reception thru to the product, branding is defined by the company's collective response to its marketplace.

The best companies continue to evolve, they out innovate their competition, and always aspire towards simple business truths: Do what you say you are going to do, Be on time, Finish what you start and always say please and thank you. Over time some companies are for whatever reason lead astray and forget the simplicity of basic business acumen. Over time consumer tastes may change. In some instances accumulated brand fatigue will inspire change.

These are the opportunities for true brand re-invention. As brand mongers, it's our task to understand what is all that the company is and what it wants to be globally. We must ensure that - in the majority - the end consumer will engage in the story the brand has to tell. We must ensure that we have distilled the company essence to it's simplest visual form. In the best cases we will invent a visual identity that encompasses an entire brand language where every communication element is easily recognized and associated with it's parent. The best brands are brands supported from within. A visual re-branding exercise inspires change through a refocusing of the business strategy and the revitalization of the employee base towards a more unified goal, when this occurs and you have consistency in product and delivery the company will resonate with inspired "brancvangelismTM", a spurious form of viral word of mouth marketing that is energized and virtually unstoppable.

Eric Sweet
Chief Creative Officer
Scribbiers' Club
Ontario, Canada

Antonin Juracka (Czech Republic)

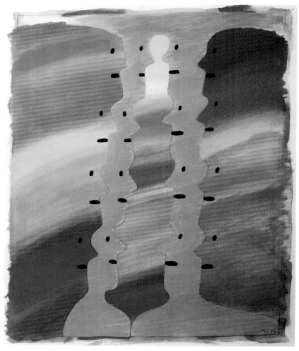

Antonin Juracka is a great artist from Czech. He has provided numerous Branding Elements for many companies internationally. He loves humankind and love. In 1995 Japan had a big earthquake in the Kobe city area. As soon as he got the news he offered to donate all of his due payments immediately through ICO.

His themes are always about love. He draws people with human race love. Unfortunately we had to say a painful farewell in March 2005 to this great Czech artist.

......With love and respect for Antonin.   ......From all of us at ICO.

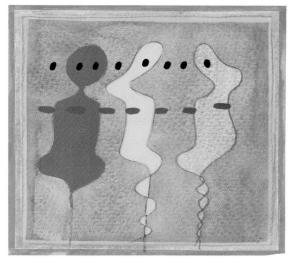

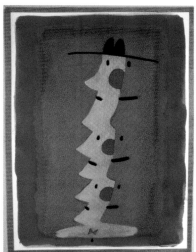

1

2

G U I M A R Ã E S

PATRIMÓNIO MUNDIAL DA HUMANIDADE

3

ESTORIL & SINTRA
CONVENTION BUREAU

4

TIP

5

ICAM

6

Instituto Português de Museus

7

Museu do **D**ouro

8

Alto Douro Vinhateiro

9

Dr. Pinto Leite
INSTITUTO DE RADIOLOGIA

10

13

11

12

Ideias Virtuais

13

Cor da Imagem

14

Loja das Ideias

15

 CASA MUNICIPAL DA JUVENTUDE

16

17

Museu do Sítio

20

19

desgrippes gobé (Brussels)
Mimosas 44
B-1030 Brussels - Belgium
Phone: + 32 2 215 34 00
Fax: + 32 2 215 39 11
Mail: info@dga.be
www.dgbrussels.be
Mr Jean J. Evrard
jjevrard@dga.be

desgrippes gobé (Hong Kong)
Unit 01, 20/F, 9 Leighton Road
Causeway Bay, Hong Kong
Phone: + 852 3106 8722
Fax: + 852 3106 0991
Mr Craig Briggs
email: cbriggs@dga.com.hk

desgrippes gobé (New York)
411 Lafayette Street New York
NY 10003 - U.S.A.
Phone: + 1 212 979 89 00
Fax: + 1 212 979 14 01
Mail: info@dga.com

desgrippes gobé (Paris)
18 bis, av. de la Motte-Picquet
75007 Paris - France
Phone: + 33 1 44 18 44 18
Fax: + 33 1 45 51 96 60
Mr François Caratgé
Mail: fcaratge@desgrippes-gobe.com

desgrippes gobé (Seoul)
Daedong B/D # 403, 587-21 Shinsa-dong,
Kangnam-ku, Seoul 135-892, Korea
Phone: + 82 2 543 5730
Fax: + 82 2 543 57 31
Ms Haejung Park
Mail: hjpark@dga.co.kr

desgrippes gobé (Shanghai)
Unit 3541, 35/F, Citic Square
1168 Nanjing Road West,
Shanghai 200041, China
Phone: + 86 21 5111 9073
Fax: + 86 21 5111 9076
Ms Helen Lai
Mail: hlai@dga.com.hk

desgrippes gobé (Tokyo)
Ebisu East 438 Building 2F
4-3-8 Ebisu Shibuya-ku
Tokyo 150-0013 - Japan
Phone: + 81 3 5791 4418
Fax: + 81 3 5791 44 20
Mr Koichi Furusawa
Mail: k.furusawa@dga.co.jp

Group publications:

www.passion4brands.com

1

ZENOAQ

2

武蔵野大学
MUSASHINO UNIVERSITY

3

Promena

4

China Media Group

5

6

19

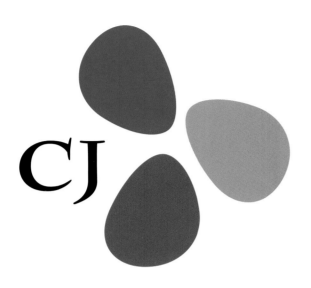

7

8

9

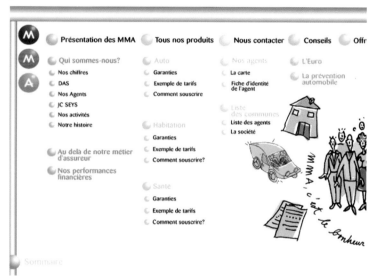

1 Client: LG
Brand: can u
Market: Japan

2 Client: Nihon Zenyaky Kogyo
Brand: Zenoaq
Market: Japan

3 Client: Musashino University
Market: Japan

4 Client: Morgan Stanley Japan
Brand: Promena (Retail Centre)
Market: Japan

5 Client: China Radio, Film and Television Group
Brand: CMG
Market: China PRC

6 Brand: Miocell
Market: Korea

7 Client: Cheil Jedang Corporation
Market: Korea

8 Client: Groupe Crédit Agricole
Brand: Sofinco
Market: France

9 Client: MAA
Market: France

10

11

12

13

14

15

16

 Electrabel

10 Client: Recticel
Brand: Beka
Market: Europe

11 Client: Brussels Airport
Brand: Sky Shops
Market: Belgium

12 Client: Promedia (Yellow Pages)
Brand: Pages d'Or
Market: Belgium

13 Client: Adecco
Brand: Ajilon
Market: World

14 Client: Marly Automotive
Brand: Marly
Market: Europe

15 Client: Tunisian Tourism Office
Market: World

16 Client: Suez Group
Brand: Electrabel
Market: Europe

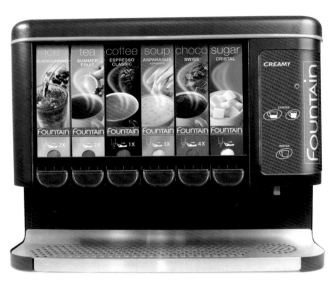

17

18

19

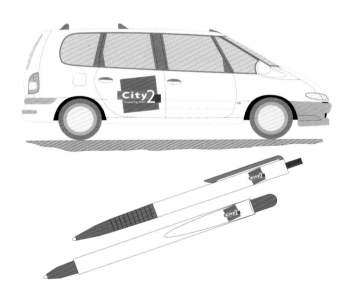

tridimage

3D PACKAGING IMAGE DESIGN
w w w . t r i d i m a g e . c o m

Tridimage is an integrated graphic and structural packaging design firm, based in Buenos Aires, Argentina. We have been producing creative and distinctive branding solutions for clients worldwide since 1995, helping them to build highly profitable wine, beverage, spirit, food and product brands.

Our extensive experience designing branding projects for clients based in countries around the globe gives us the know-how necessary for the smooth running of global design projects from large to small.

We work with a wide range of international clients within a variety of industries. The ongoing and intensely collaborative relationships that we form with our clients give us the opportunity to work with them on focused projects as well as on their long-term communication strategies. When strong 3D creativity is grounded in thoughtful, forward-looking strategy, the result is surpased client expectations, and superior satisfaction for our clients' customer.

1 Haraszthy Vallejo Pincészet
   Hungarian wines

2 The e-Commerce company
Patagonian Life
Dulce de Leche

CUSENIER

3

Prima
LABORATORIOS

4

A·G·L·H
PREMIUM

5

ALL NATURAL

GOLDEN
ANDES

6

HENRY
GRAN GUARDA

7

BODEGAS ALVEAR

Federico de Alvear

8

3 Pernod Ricard Argentina
Cusenier
Liqueurs

4 Laboratorios Prima
Laboratory

5 AGLH
Premium Honey

6 Expanding Frontiers
Golden Andes
Olive Oil

7 Lagarde
Henry
Premium wines

8 J. Llorente
Federico de Alvear
Wines and Sparklings

dragonFLY

9

COMPAÑÍA
PREMIER

10

11

m-products

12

13

LIPPINCOTT MERCER

Lippincott Mercer is a leading design and brand strategy consultancy. The firm has an enviable track record in helping to solve the most complex branding challenges facing corporations today. That track record is driven by an understanding of the art and science of branding, a disciplined process, deep experience and the hands-on approach of senior partners.

As a result, Lippincott helps clients become better known and better understood, and helps create preference for their products and services through the successful creation, valuation and management of their brands.

Lippincott was founded in 1943 as Lippincott & Margulies and is part of Marsh & McLennan Companies, Inc. Lippincott operates globally from its headquarters in New York City and other offices in the United States, Europe, Asia and Latin America.

For more information
lippincottmercer.com
info@lm.mmc.com

New York
Lippincott Mercer
499 Park Avenue
New York, NY 10022
United States
Tel +1 212 521 0000
Fax +1 212 754 2591

London
Lippincott Mercer
1 Grosvenor Place
London SW1X 7HJ
United Kingdom
Tel +44 (0)20 7915 9800
Fax +44 (0)20 7915 9801

Boston
Lippincott Mercer
200 Clarendon Street
Boston, MA 02116
United States
Tel +1 617 424 3200
Fax +1 617 424 3701

Hong Kong
Lippincott Mercer
32nd Floor RBS Tower
Times Square
One Matheson Street
Causeway Bay
Hong Kong
Tel +852 2506 0767
Fax +852 2506 4478

Nissan Motors' global brand revitalization is taking a major step forward in the U.S. with the introduction of a new Retail Environmental Design Program for all its dealerships. To accomplish this, Nissan's brand integration team partnered with Lippincott Mercer to create a unique retail presentation that would provide an optimal environment for the merchandising of Nissan vehicles, accessories and services, while reflecting the company's new brand identity.

agere ^{systems}

Catapult Learning

Bancroft
NeuroHealth

CENDANT

cognistar

Continental

ExxonMobil

Holland+Knight

HOUSEHOLD

When **Time Warner** decided to drop AOL from the parent corporation name, Lippincott Mercer was asked to create the new visual identity. The new logotype was designed to echo the company's classic look of the past, but in a refreshed design. The graphic rules above and below the name were eliminated to reduce the look and feel of an old masthead. The new typeface selected for the logotype is a classic Bodoni and the color is a royal blue. The result is a refreshed and elegant new corporate identity.

INFINITI

plural

JohnsonDiversey

Sabre

Scripps

SAMSUNG

SONIC

TELUS

مؤسسة سلطان بن عبد العزيز آل سعود الخيرية
SULTAN BIN ABDULAZIZ AL-SAUD FOUNDATION

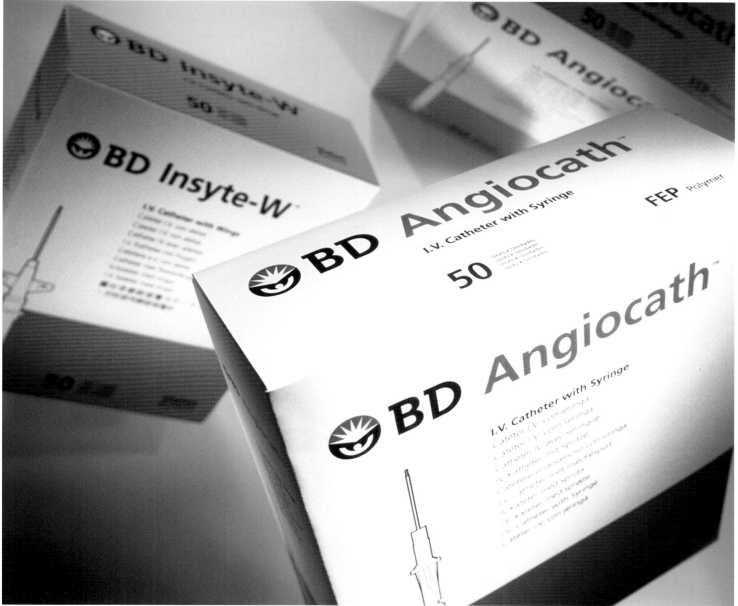

When **Becton Dickinson**, a $3 billion medical devices company was in the midst of a cultural transformation. The leadership of the company recognized the need to communicate more effectively to customers and other audiences. Lippincott Mercer developed new identity guidelines, branding standards and implementation plans to ensure that the new program continues to support the company's goals and purpose: "to help all people live healthy lives."

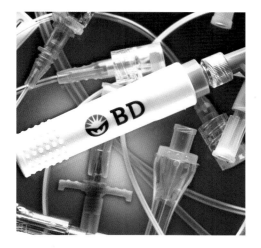

Russell Leong Design (USA)

RLD — COMPANY **Russell Leong Design** — MADE IN U.S.A.

ADDRESS
847 Emerson Street / Palo Alto, California 94301 / USA

TELECOMMUNICATIONS
Tel 650.321.2443 / Fax 650.321.5429 / Email eighty88@aol.com

URL
russellleong.com

Russell Leong Design is a graphic design firm based in Palo Alto, California. It was established by owner and principal, Russell K. Leong.

Specializing in corporate communications, corporate graphic design and sales program materials, from research through a wide range of needs and applications. Other capabilities include packaging design, brochures, annual reports, signage, etc.

A highly respected and well-known design firm, Russell Leong Design has worked with many prominent clients both locally and nationally including Symantec Corporation, Visa International, Inc. and Sun Microsystems, Inc.

Russell Leong Design has won numerous awards from art directors clubs and graphic design associations including The American Institute of Graphic Arts, The New York Art Directors Club, The Houston Art Directors Clubs, The Art Directors Club of Los Angeles, and the Western Art Directors Club. RLD's work is also represented in the collection of the Library of Congress. Work done by the office has appeared in various design publications including Communication Arts, Graphis/Self promotion, How Magazine, Step magazine, Dynamic Graphics, Novum, and Print Regional Annual.

Russell Leong has lectured for many years in graphic design at California State University/San Jose State University, Academy of Art University and at the University of California, Santa Cruz Extension Program.

1 1. Solaris 10 / SUN MICROSYSTEMS, INC.
2. Sun Microsystems product branding

2 1. Andalé Mexican Restaurant & Bar
2. Mexican restaurant

3 1. Dr. Martin Luther King, Jr. Library / CITY OF SAN JOSÉ / SAN JOSÉ STATE UNIVERSITY
2. Public library

A N N I E G L A S S

OneWorld™
s y s t e m s

4 1. Annieglass
   2. Designer / manufacturer of fine dinnerware / glassware

7 1. OneWorld Systems / GLOBAL VILLAGE, INC.
   2. Manufacturer of communication servers

POCKET

5 1. WhoWhere? / LYCOS, INC.
   2. Internet search engine product branding

8 1. 5 Pocket / L'UOMO INTERNATIONAL
   2. Contemporary clothing retail store

ICONIX
PHARMACEUTICALS

bistro
S H I K U M E N

法 藍 極 梠

6 1. Iconix Pharmaceuticals
   2. Chemogenomics / biotech developer / manufacturer

9 1. Shikumen Bistro / NEW CHINA RESTNTURES, LLC
   2. French-mediterranean restaurant

10 1. 8 1/2 / L'UOMO INTERNATIONAL
2. Women's retail shoe store

13 1. Rice Paper / RICE PAPER, INC.
2. Manufacturer and distributor of asian paper goods

11 1. Department of Geography / UNIVERSITY OF CALIFORNIA, BERKELEY
2. Commemorative branding for department anniversary

14 1. Rad Pad / RADICAL CONCEPTS, INC.
2. Manufacturer and distributor of luxury seating products

12 1. Symantec / SYMANTEC, INC.
2. Software manufacturer

BRUCE LEE: A RETROSPECTIVE

15 1. Bruce Lee / CHINESE CULTURE FOUNDATION/SF
2. Event branding for retrospective exhibition

16 1. Eyecandy / ANNIEGLASS
    2. Jewelry / clothing retail store

17 1. Palo Alto Art Center / CITY OF PALO ALTO
    2. Municipal art center facility

18 1. Turner Martin / TURNER MARTIN, INC
    2. Retail home furnishings store

19 1. Symantec Achievers Trip / SYMANTEC, INC.
    2. Sales group incentive event branding

20 1. Betelnut / REAL RESTAURANTS, INC.
    2. Pan-Asian restaurant

21 1. Richardson Architects
    2. Architectural firm

22 1. Visa International Hong Kong 1992 / VISA INTERNATIONAL
2. Event branding / Annual meeting in Hong Kong

25 1. Live365.com
2. Media-rich music internet

23 1. Shanghai 1930 / GQC HOLDINGS, INC.
2. Asian restaurant / private club

26 1. CareSoft / CARESOFT, INC.
2. Internet healthcare management software

24 1. Mobile Computing Division / HEWLETT-PACKARD
2. Internal product branding for notebook computer division

27 1. Bing Towerhouse Project / STANFORD UNIVERSITY
2. Event / project branding

28 1. Ming's Chinese Cuisine and Bar
2. Asian restaurant

31 1. Kiva Genetics
2. Human genome research company

29 1. Programmers Press / IDG BOOKS WORLDWIDE, INC.
2. Publisher of computer books

32 1. Black & White Ball / CITY OF PALO ALTO
2. Logotype for city fundraising event

30 1. Diddams Amazing Party Stores
2. Purveyor of party supplies

33 1. CountryLife / NUTRITIONAL SUPPLEMENTS, INC.
2. Manufacturer of nutritional and lifestyle products

34 1. Parallel Tasking / 3COM CORPORATION
2. Ethernet technology product branding

37 1. Blu / L'UOMO INTERNATIONAL
2. Retail women's apparel store

35 1. Roti / REAL RESTAURANTS, INC.
2. Wood-fired rotisserie restaurant

38 1. CAP / CENTRAL AVENUE PHARMACY
2. Compounding pharmacy

36 1. ComputerMania / SOFTBANK EXPOS
2. Family computing trade show

39 1. E Three / E-MU SYSTEMS, INC.
2. Digital sampling keyboard product branding

40 1. Achievers Trip 2000 / SYMANTEC, INC.
2. Sales group incentive event branding

MaskTools®

41 1. MaskTools / MICROUNITY, INC.
2. Product / technology branding

42 1. Prophet / PROPHET FINANCIAL GROUP
2. Stock trading internet portal

43 1. Graffiti Busters / CITY OF PALO ALTO
2. Graffiti abatement program branding

44 1. ReleaseNow
2. e-business software for software manufacturers

45 1. Guai Guai / OOLONG TEES, INC.
2. Manufacturer of Asian lifestyle apparel

COLON INCA / Graphic Arts / Spain

PALMA PAN / Bakery Company / Spain

PEIXINHO / Restaurant Sheraton / Portugal

CATA Goumet / Delicatessen / Spain

UVIPE / Wine Company / Spain

LECIÑENA / Transport company / Spain

ACDHA / Company for Alimentary Hygiene / Spain

ASALIMEN / importers of Spanish Food / USA

RELLMAN FOODS / Ecological Food Importers /
Belgium

INSTAPAN / Bakery Company / Spain

45

OROTANA / Mineral Water / Spain

FUENSANTA / Mineral Water / Spain

G.I. / Architects and Designers / England

IFA / Financial Assesment / Kuwait

COSA / Building Company / Spain

GOLF & COUNTRY CLUB / Sheraton / Portugal

EURO PAN / Bakery Company / USA

GALEA / Mineral Water / Spain

KIH / Housing Investment Company / Kuwait

GREEN PAMPA / Meet Importers / Belgium

GUSI BEJER / Illustrator / Spain

STANG

STANG (The Netherlands)

Ideograma (México)

Juan Carlos Fernández Espinosa
Director Creativo

ideograma

t: (777) 313 8466   ext. 101
jc@ideograma.com
Priv. Puerto Escondido 18
Fracc.Bugambilias
Cuernavaca, México 62140-4
www.ideograma.com

IDEAS CON IDENTIDAD

"hola"

Ideograma is a Mexican consultancy that captures the ideas floating in the air so they can be shaped through reminiscent and outstanding corporate identities, helping our clients to reveal their uniqueness and authenticity within a creative and moving "global" identity.

To communicate that we are a transparent, flexible and innovative firm, we developed an identity with multiple symbols by means of a green balloon ("globo" in Spanish) transformed into different animals that convey the personality of the application they represent.

Pastelandia
La felicidad de compartir

1

RETO *tu reencuentro*

2

1 Pastelandia
   A decorative meringue flower
   promotes "the happiness of
   sharing" for this pastry shop.

2 Reto
   Foundation to support women
   with suspicion or diagnosis of
   breast cancer.

3 Lifestyles
   The "tree of life" celebrates the
   abundance and diversity of this
   furniture store.

4 Aliados Contra la Piratería
   The "pirate mark" confronts us
   when we wound the personal
   and the authentic.

5 Escalera Náutica
   The biodiversity in the infinite
   encounters between ocean and
   desert of Mexico's sustainable
   tourist development in the
   Sea of Cortez.

6 Markus tecno logics
   The *aurora borealis* weaves the
   wireless communication web of
   this Scandinavian company.

LIFESTYLES
HABITAT

3

4

ESCALERA NÁUTICA
del Mar de Cortés

5

Markus
tecno logics

6

Lluvia de ideas

Contigo
es posible

*aster

Fundación
Comunidad

the
Anglo

7 Lluvia de ideas
   Imagine what one drop of
   creativity from this consultancy
   ("Brainstorming" in Spanish) can
   spark off in your organization.

8 Contigo
   An emblem with the hands that
   give shape to Mexico for the
   governmental social programs.

9 *aster
   Name and symbol fusion in
   this innovative entertainment
   company in Dominican
   Republic.

10 Comunidad
   The empty space invites us to
   sow our own seed in alliance
   with this Mexican Community
   Foundation.

11 The Anglo
   The Mexican-British bicultural
   encounter is represented through
   an Aztec glyph and a band
   based on St. George's cross.

PUBLICIDAD
VIRTUAL

impulso

12

13

12 Publicidad Virtual
The marble marvels us with
the magic and transparency
of virtual product placement.

13 Impulso
This financial society offers
a guaranty credit to give
the necessary impulse to
your dreams.

14 AMCO
The pre-Hispanic symbol of
communication is formed
with real silhouettes of their
members while they exchange
ideas and experiences.

15 Hábitat
An urban development program
contributes to "build a city" and
create spaces with social identity
and value.

16 Luxury Avenue
A mall-boutique in Cancun
reunites the best luxury brands
from the world.

17 Ultrafemme
An ethereal and feminine ribbon
decorates the biggest Mexican
perfume seller.

ASOCIACIÓN MEXICANA DE COMUNICADORES

AMCO

14

Hábitat

15

LUXURY AVENUE

16

Ultrafemme

17

alamah

 ESOTERISMO
 VISUAL
 TRADICIONES DE ORIENTE
 NATURISMO
 ESPIRITUALIDAD
 CLÁSICOS
 MEDICINA ALTERNATIVA
 AUTOAYUDA

18

Latido

19

HECHIZOS ESENCIALES

20

REDES
Marcas con Estrategia

Enlace

21

22

18 Alamah
The "halo" integrates the different collections of this publisher house in a unique identity system.

19 Latido
This Dominican foundation helps kids with heart diseases.

20 Hechizos Esenciales
Hand-made soaps with essential oils that come to life by fusioning earth, air, water and fire.

21 Redes
This consultancy inserted at the center of the social framework uses concentrical images of natural networks.

22 Enlace
The first Mexican interbanking brokerage company mediates fair and equal transactions between its two "Exchangers".

Born 20 years ago with the concept of combining strategy and creation into design,
dragon rouge is the leading independent design company in the world.

"Creative, Passionate, Entrepreneurial!"
dragon rouge, the n°1 design consultancy in France and among the top 5 in Europe with offices
in Paris, Hamburg, London, New York and Warsaw, is a team of 260 creative designers and
consultants who partner with their clients to develop strong, long-lasting and unique brands to
keep them, at all times, one step ahead of their competitors.

Through branding and packaging, dragon rouge has a threefold mission :
1- Revitalizing long-established brands to provide them with even greater permanence.
2- Stimulating brands to make them central to our lives and constantly renew their ties with
   consumers.
3- Innovating to prepare the brands of today to be the leading brands of tomorrow.

dragon rouge
32, rue Pagès
BP 83 92153
F-92152 Suresnes Cedex
Tel. 33 -1- 46 97 50 00
Fax. 33 -1- 46 97 50 80
www.dragonrouge.com

1 Acqua Panna (Sanpellegrino S.p.A., Nestlé) - International
Promotion of the brand's historical strengths and, in particular, its Tuscan origins to make it a major classic chosen to grace the very best gourmet restaurants around the world.

2 Maille olive oil (Unilever) - International
In accordance with the graphic codes specific to the Maille brand, creation of an up-market graphic message to express the exceptional quality and Mediterranean origins of a first cold-pressed olive oil.

3 Lipton Ice Tea (Unilever) - International
For the n°1 producer of iced tea worldwide, creation of a brand identity and packaging design that correspond to the visual codes of the world of soft drinks, to gain in modernity and reinforce the central promise of "natural refreshment".

4 LU (Danone) - International
Unification of the range of biscuits sold in 47 non European Countries through a design that highlights the origin of the biscuits while positioning them as a premium and gourmet offer.

1 Dubonnet (Pernod-Ricard) - International
Dubonnet, the famous—indeed, mythical—brand of traditional French aperitif created in 1846 by Joseph Dubonnet, reverts back to the avant-garde vision of its creator who chose to associate his brand with a single powerful icon: the cat.

2 Cointreau (Rémy-Cointreau) - International
Reinforcement of the durability of the brand and its values through a new brand identity, a more refined label, a new medallion and an emphasis of the copper colour code on the stopper.

3 Wyborowa (Pernod-Ricard) - International
For Poland's most celebrated vodka, the
reassertion of its authenticity derived from
500 years of tradition through a more
elegantly shaped bottle, more up-to-date
graphic codes and a specific icon engraved
on the glass to evoke the traditional distilling
techniques used in the production process.

4 Martell (Pernod Ricard) - International
VS : creation of a seasonal packaging for
one of the most dynamic brands of Cognac
Cordon Bleu : Revitalization of a major
success brand in Asia.

1 Nivea (Beiersdorf) - Europe
Creation of 3D and graphic design of the range of bath care products (shower & bath gels) to reassert the strong position enjoyed by Nivea in that segment, and to communicate the specific qualities of each of the products more effectively while simultaneously respecting the general values of gentleness and respect of the individual conveyed by the brand.

2 Le Petit Marseillais (Laboratoires Vendôme) - France
The front-ranking player in the market for shower gels, bubble baths and soap in France, Le Petit Marseillais commands a unique positioning based on the theme of the Mediterranean and Provence conveyed by transparent packaging combined with true, natural colours.

3 Press Kit Christian Dior Iod (LVMH) - Europe
Creation of a graphic environment for the publication of the various documents designed to accompany the launch of a new Christian Dior perfume in the press.

4 Samsara de Guerlain (LVMH) - International
For Samsara, one of the most well known perfumes produced by Guerlain, new 3D design of the bottle to convey greater refinement, and a new emphasis on the texture of the materials used for the box to conjure up the feel and shimmer of silk.

5 Rituals - Europe
Launch of a new range of more than 150 products to bridge the gap between two different worlds—personal hygiene and household cleanliness—offering to transform everyday "routines" into meaningful ritual gestures.

Guerrini Design Island (Argentina)

Sebastian Guerrini is designer in Visual Communication, Postgrade in Communications Tecnologies and Master in Image Studies.

Sebastian Guerrini was born in 1965. He studied in Argentina, The Netherlands and England. At present he is finishing his PhD in Image Studies, researching at the University of Kent on the link between national identity and image.

He has carried out image and identity design work in Latin America, Spain, Italy, Ireland and England. In Argentina, he designed, among other jobs, the present visual identity of the National Presidency, Ministries and State Secretary Offices and the CONICET, together with the current version of the Argentine National Shield.

He has worked for the National State, provincial states and town halls, with organisations such as United Nations, Amnesty International, UNICEF, Latin American Social Science Council, and Pan American Health Organization. At his studio he has designed for banks, consultancies, universities, schools, products and their respective identity applications, such as the Grupo Los Grobo, one of the most important agribusiness companies of Argentina.

Additionally, he has taught Postgraduate courses, Seminars and Conferences in Argentina and abroad.

1-2 National Council of Scientific and Technologic Investigations, the National Agency for Scientific and Technologic Promotion, and the National Secretary of Science, Technology and Productive Innovation.
Visual identity design
Argentina, 2004

3 Argentinean Industrial Sectors
Visual identity design
Argentina, 2004

4-5-6 National Presidency, Ministries and State Secretary Offices
Visual identity design
Design of the current version of the Argentine National Shield

1

2

3

5

6

7

8

9

7 OSAL
*Latin American Council
for Social Sciences*

8 Serra Maiori Cultural Meeting
Visual identity design
Italy

9 Latin America Meeting (United Nations)
Visual identity design

10

11

10 **Marina Studios**
   Visual identity design
   Ireland, 2004

11 **Societat Orgànica**
   Visual identity design
   Barcelona, Spain, 2004

12 **Bioceres**
   Visual identity design
   Argentina, 2004

13 **Grupo Los Grobo**
   Visual identity design
   Argentina, 2004

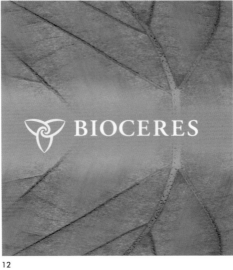

12

13

14

14 Culture Secretary of the
Argentine Nation
Poster design
*Memorial to the victims
of the Holocaust*
Argentina, 2000

15 Culture Secretary of the
Argentine Nation
Poster design
*National Awards of Literature,
Music and Theatre*
Argentina, 2000

16 Culture Secretary of the
Argentine Nation
Promotion of the
Literature Culture
Argentina, 2001

15

16

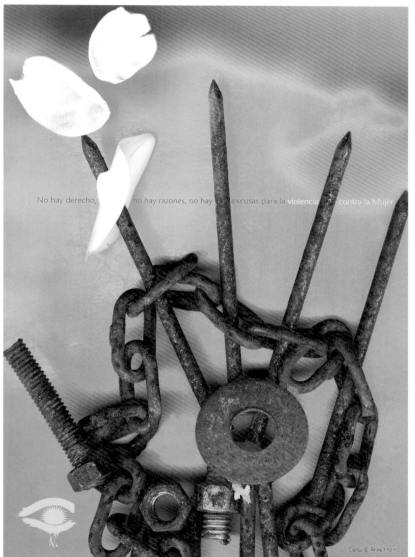

No hay derecho, no hay razones, no hay excusas para la violencia contra la Mujer

17

17-18 Women National Council (Argentina), UNICEF,
Pan American Health Organization, BID, Unifem
Campaign against violence on women
"There is no reason, no excuse, no right for violence against woman"
Argentina, 2001

18

Minale Tattersfield & Partners

Minale Tattersfield & Partners is an international design consultancy with a reputation based on both excellent standards of creativity and the commercial success of its designs.

Offering the benefits of 40 years experience, the company has an impressive portfolio and prides itself on many long-standing client relationships.

The London studio heads a network of design agencies across the world and is a pioneer in design for global markets.

With over 300 international awards and nine books under its belt, **Minale Tattersfield & Partners** is ranked amongst the top ten design agencies by the Financial Times, Design Week and Marketing.

Minale Tattersfield & Partners
London Head Office: The Poppy Factory, 20 Petersham Road, Richmond, Surrey TW10 6UR UK
Tel: +44 20 8948 7999 - Fax: +44 20 8948 2435 - Email:mtp@mintat.co.uk - Website: www.mintat.co.uk

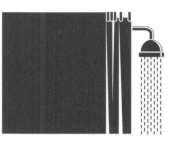

SCAFFALI

GIARDINAGGIO

ARREDO DA BAGNO

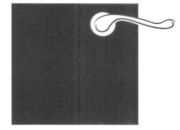

FERRAMENTA

MANIGLIE

VERNICI

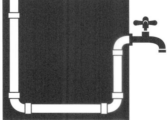

1

LEGNO

IDRAULICA

1
Brico
Branding, signage and identity

Minale Tattersfield & Partners was commissioned to enhance the image of Brico Center, Italy's largest chain of DIY stores. Brico had recognized that to refresh its identity was essential to support its position as the leading DIY Company in Italy.

Minale Tattersfield & Partners researched, repositioned the company; then detailed, implemented and supervised the reimaging programme.

Our graphic designers restyled the familiar Brico logotype by creating a more contemporary image whilst increasing the amount of red in the logo giving Brico "ownership" of red - a dynamic and highly visible colour.

The key manifestation of the project was to provide Brico's customers with a clear signage system that would aid orientation as well as provide them with useful information. The design style adopted was a contemporary and friendly look with good visibility.

Another key consideration for a cost-effective design was the number of stores to which the store fascias would be applied. Minale Tattersfield & Partners multi-disciplinary team rigorously considered the implication of every recommendation from a wide range of viewpoints intended to give added value by satisfying consumer, client and staff needs.

To ensure consistency of application of the new identity, we devised and implemented a corporate visual standards manual.

1

2

1 Colombina
Complete rebranding programme

Colombina was born as a producer of candies, its visual image dating back some seventy years. Initially, Colombina was present only in Colombia with few competitors.

Today Colombina is a multinational company with a global presence. The company felt the existing identity along with its product brands to be outdated and out of touch with todays consumer and the multitude of choice being offered to them.

The solution was to totally refresh the existing over-complicated Colombina logo, and replace with a more dynamic and forward looking design. Likewise existing product brand identities were redesigned and all packaging ranges brought together under a clearly structured packaging architecture, reinforcing the brand recognition.

The new identity carries an extensive corporate identity manual for all applications at corporate and consumer level.

3

2 Colombina
Redesigned packaging ranges

Demonstrating the new direction.

3 Colombina
Bon Bon Bum logo

Colombina's brand leader.

4

4 Colombina
Bon Bon Bum lollipops packaging range

The brand carries many different flavours, with new ones continually being developed and launched. They are sold throughout supermarkets, corner shops, and street vendors. The new brand architecture facilitates a coordinated look, whilst individual creative freedom is permitted for different flavours.

1 Rizzoli
Branding, signage and identity

Rizzoli is one of Italy's leading bookstores. When they opened a chain of franchised stores under the new name Rizzoli Store, they commissioned Minale Tattersfield & Partners to design the identity and sign system.

The identity focuses on the 'O' of Rizzoli applied horizontally as opposed to vertically. In this way both Rizzoli and Store are attributed equal importance and it serves to differentiate the group from the original Rizzoli book shops.

The colours project a youthful and contemporary image. The 'O' has been used for external signage, labels, bags, T-shirts and door handles.

The sign system is based on the two colours orange and grey. Grey is used to depict services such as information points and toilets. Orange is used for the different book categories throughout the store.

THE BARRIE TUCKER COMPANY (Australia)

Memberships:
AGI (Alliance Graphique Internationale)
LFDIA (Life Fellow, Design Institute of Australia)

Publications:
'The Design World of Barrie Tucker', Tokyo, 1991 (Japan)

Feature Articles:
'Graphis' magazine, Issues 190 (including cover),
266 (USA)
'Graphis' Design Annual, 1993 (USA)
'Identity' magazine, Issue Winter '89 (USA)
'AXIS' Magazine, Issue 43 (Japan)
'Who's Who In Graphic Design' First Edition 1982,
Second Edition 1994 (Switzerland)
'Graphis' Bottle Design, 1997 (USA)
'Critique' magazine, 1997 (USA)

Exhibitions:
'L'Etiquette de Vin' Exhibition, Lausanne (Switzerland) 1990
'The Design World of Barrie Tucker', AXIS Gallery, Tokyo, (Japan)
December,1991
'World Peace Flag' Exhibition, Polish Pavilion, World Expo '92,
Seville (Spain) 1992
'Three Australians', Galerie Von Oertzen, Frankfurt
(Germany) 1992
'Gitanes, Silhouette' Exhibition, Georges Pompidou Centre, Paris
(France) 1996
'World Environment Poster' Exhibition, (UNFCCC – COP3), Kyoto
(Japan) 1997
'The World of Graphic Design', Frankfurt (Germany) 1997 & Essen
(Germany) 1998

Collections:
Icograda Permanent Collection, London (England)
Museum for Arts and Crafts, Hamburg (Germany)
German Poster Museum, Essen (Germany)
'People to People' collage/mural, UNESCO World Headquarters,
Paris (France)
Powerhouse Museum, Sydney (Australia)
IOC (International Olympic Committee) Museum, Lausanne
(Switzerland)
Bibliotheque Nationale de France (National Library of France),
Paris (France)
San Francisco Museum of Modern Art, San Francisco (USA)

Major Awards:
3 Merit Awards for Publication Design, The New York Art Directors
Club 1972-1974 (USA)
11 Awards of Excellence for Publications, Illustration and Packaging
Design,
Communication Arts, 1973-1990 (USA)
President's Award, Adelaide Art Directors Club,
1979 (Australia)
The Gold Chair Award, Adelaide Art Directors Club,
1981, 1987 (Australia)
Gold Medal for Brochure Design, Australian National Print Awards,
1986 (Australia)
3 Silver Pencil Awards, 1 Bronze Pencil Award for Packaging
Design, AWARD (Australian Writers and Art Directors), 1986-1988
(Australia)

8 Certificates of Honour for Wine Packaging Design,
CLIO Awards, 1986-1991 (USA)
3 Gold and 2 Silver CLIO Statuettes for Wine Packaging Design,
1995, 1996 (USA)
First Prize, International Cultural Section, Lahti Poster Biennale,
1987 (Finland)
4 Silver Awards for Typography and Corporate Identity,
Typographers International Association Awards,
1988, 1989 (USA)
3 Certificates of Excellence, 'Best Trademarks of the Eighties',
Washington Trademark Design Awards, 1990 (USA)
Grand Prize for Packaging Design, Gold Star and Silver Star for
Wine Packaging Design, Australian National Packaging Awards,
1990, 2000 (Australia)
Gold Medal for Wine Labels, Australian National Print Awards,
1993 (Australia)
2 Pinnacle Awards for Design Excellence/Best of Category,
Publication Design, Packaging Design, Australian Graphic Design
Association,1994, 1996 (Australia)
World Star Pack Award, International Packaging Awards, 1995
(England)

Design Juries:
New York Art Directors Club International Awards,
New York (USA) 1991
Australia Post, Stamp Advisory Committee, Melbourne (Australia)
1996-2001
Australian Graphic Design Association Awards, Adelaide (Australia)
2002

Major Lectures:
'Barrie Tucker Design Dreams', AGDA Lecture Series, Brisbane
(Australia) 1998
'Barrie Tucker Speaks Design', AGDA Lecture Series, Canberra
(Australia) 1999
'Barrie Tucker in the Hunter Valley', AGDA Lecture Series, Pokolbin
(Australia) 1999
'AGIdeas', International Design Conference, Melbourne (Australia)
2001

The Barrie Tucker Company

105/117 North Road, Nairne

South Australia 5252

Postal Address:

PO Box 390, Nairne

South Australia 5252

+61 8 8388 0236

barrie@barrietucker.com

www.barrietucker.com

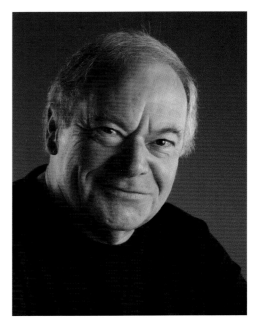

1. 1 Greenway Architects
2 Brand identity logotype made up of architectural graphic icons symbolising the many design aspects of an architectural practice
3 Brand identity used on plans, stationery, office building and site signage

2. 1 Seaford
2 Brand identity presentation projects a healthy, sunny and bright lifestyle for this seaside residential development
3 Brand identity used on stationery, sales literature, sales office signs and flags, site signs and large advertising poster sites

1

2

3. 1   Sanctuary Cove Resort
     2   Country Club signage provides a quality, sculptural presence at the front entry
        to the exclusive Club

3

4. 1 McLaren Vale and Fleurieu Visitor Centre
2 Brand identity presented as signage unit at the front entry to the Visitor Centre situated
at the gateway to this South Australian wine growing and tourism district
3 Brand identity used on stationery, promotion materials, wine packaging and
merchandise articles

4

5. 1   Burton Premium Wines
   2   Brand identity created exclusively for a marketer of quality Australian wine.
     The photograph shows the brand identity presentation created for the company's
     premium red wine and features the icon embossed on the shoulder of the bottle
   3   Brand identity used on stationery and promotional material. The paper used for
     labels, stationery and promotion materials was a pseudo parchment style

6. 1   ARH Australia Wine Company
   2   Brand identity created for the wine company's premium 'Clarendon' red wine and shown
     as used on the embossed bottle and label. The embossed logo/brand on the shoulder
     of the bottle has been sandblasted to provide an exclusive cameo look and feel of quality

5

6

7. 1   Yalumba Wine Company
    2   Logotype and illustration forming the brand identity for all products in the range of quality
        'Heggies' brand of Australian wines
    3   Brand identity was created for use on stationery, sales brochures, advertising and
        posters in addition to packaging

8. 1   Yalumba Wine Company
    2   Brand identity created for the wine company's flagship red wine 'Octavius'. The Roman
        influenced 'Octavius' icon, the blind embossed vintage date and the hand-torn base of the
        paper label add an exclusiveness to the overall presentation

7

8

2F Ebisu East 438 bldg
Shibuya-ku Tokyo 150-0013
tel: +81 3 5791 4418
fax: +81 3 5791 4420
www.dga.com

desgrippes gobé(d/g*) is a global branding and design agency, renowned for a commitment to outstanding creative solutions and widely recognised for its uniquely sensorial approach to brand design, a philosophy called "emotional branding".

d/g*'s emotional branding system is based on the belief that deep, long-lasting and successful relationships are based on powerful emotional connections. A strong brand and a strong relationship both require touching people's feelings. This means moving beyond the ordinary to create amazing experiences and moments of delight. d/g* combines creative inspiration with strategic excellence to create brands that resonate with people's intelligence, heart and intuition.

Our Tokyo office, which serves as d/g*'s Asia-Pacific regional headquarters was founded in 1991. d/g* offers clients across Asia a full range of services including brand strategy, corporate identity design, brand naming, retail architecture design, product design, and package design.

Rakuten Golden Eagles

d/g* was responsible for development of the identity for Japan's first new professional baseball team in 50 years. Our team of specialists created a great new brand and visual identity for this high profile and exciting project. The logo captures the soaring power of an eagle's spreading wings, and was followed by creation of the full identity, including mascot characters and brand tag line.

1. Client: Rakuten Baseball, Inc.
   Category: Professional Baseball team
   Production Date: 2004

Moonstar World March

The World March footwear brand was targeted at a narrow segment of walking hobbyists. d/g* was responsible for revitalising and reenergizing the brand with a strategy creating two product sub-categories: "sport walking" shoes and comfortable but fashionable "style walking" shoes. d/g* also created a technology brand "Walking Saver" to communicate the strengths of the World March product and support its premium price. Based on this brand architecture, we developed a full visual identity and logo, and applications such as packaging and retail presence.

2. Client: MoonStar chemical corp.
Category: Walking ware
Production Date: 2004

武蔵野大学
MUSASHINO UNIVERSITY

Musashino University

One of Japan's oldest Buddhist universities, Musashino University needed to clarify its role and identity in the complex educational environment of the 21st century. d/g* worked closely with a team of students and staff to develop a strategy and visual expression. Based on the concept of "connection", the identity respects Musashino's heritage while emphasising the university's contemporary mission. The dynamic energy of the logo symbolises the power of connection and process.

3. Client: Musashino University
Category: University
Production Date: 2003

Lumen (Italy)

LUMEN branding innovation

LUMEN was founded in 2003 by two of the most experienced branding experts in Italy; **Pietro Rovatti** and **Drew Smith**. Pietro Rovatti is a specialist in corporate identity and retail design, creating memorable identities that cover the whole spectrum of the "brand experience". Drew Smith is an expert in consumer branding with a track record of creating market successes for both national and international clients. Their work has won many national and international awards and has appeared in numerous publications.

Corporate identity

Successful corporate identity branding is the result of a process that mixes an analytical approach with an inspired creative process. LUMEN, thanks to an experienced team coming from the most important international agencies, is able to manage projects that originate from the brand and expand to cover multimedia, editorial, stand and retail applications. A passion for creating beautiful things, a continuous search for innovation and flexibility in executing projects are the elements that characterise LUMEN's relationships to its corporate clients.

Consumer branding

Whether it is a simple restyling or a new product development, our expertise covers all aspects of consumer branding and packaging design. We have clients in both FMCG (Fast Moving Consumer Goods) and luxury consumables. Our capabilities include concept development, naming, shape design (including CAD, prototyping and realistic model-making), identity and graphics. We guarantee that our creative proposals are feasible from a production standpoint and provide support throughout printing and implementation to ensure "on shelf" success.

Strategic and design services

Development of competitive brand strategies

Assistance in market research and trend analysis

Corporate and brand identity development

Brand management and implementation

New product development

Packaging

Naming

Retail and environmental design

Interactive media

Point of purchase and merchandising

Company communications and literature

Partial client list

Alfa Romeo - ArjoWiggins - Bauli - BPU - Breil - BTicino Consorzio Chianti Classico - Ferrarelle - Ferrero - Fiditalia Frescobaldi - Gancia - Granarolo - Henkel - Henkell & Söhnlein Iperal - Kinder - Manetti & Roberts - Monsanto - Parmalat Regional Government of Lombardy - SAB/Miller - Sagit - Spontex Stock - Yomo - Zuegg

Contact

Via Tortona 4

20144 Milan, Italy

Tel. +39 02 89 40 31 24

Fax +39 02 89 40 03 58

www.lumengroup.com

info@lumengroup.com

Member of PDA - Pan European Brand Design Association

1

1

Premio Rosa Camuna

1. Regional Government of Lombardy
2. The civic awards *Premio Rosa Camuna*
   and *Lombardia per il Lavoro*
3. Identity and communications kit

1

2

3

1 1. Regional Government of Lombardy
   2. Regional parliament building
      - Grattacielo Pirelli
   3. Brand identity and communication
      materials for various events

2 1. Fiditalia
   2. Credidea financial services
   3. Name creation and identity

3 1. Kauffmann & Sons
   2. Eagleye software
   3. Name creation and identity

4 1. Museums of Florence
   2. Exhibition *"Forme per il David"*
   3. Identity and communications kit

5 1. Illy
   2. *Università del Caffé* - Triest
   3. Identity

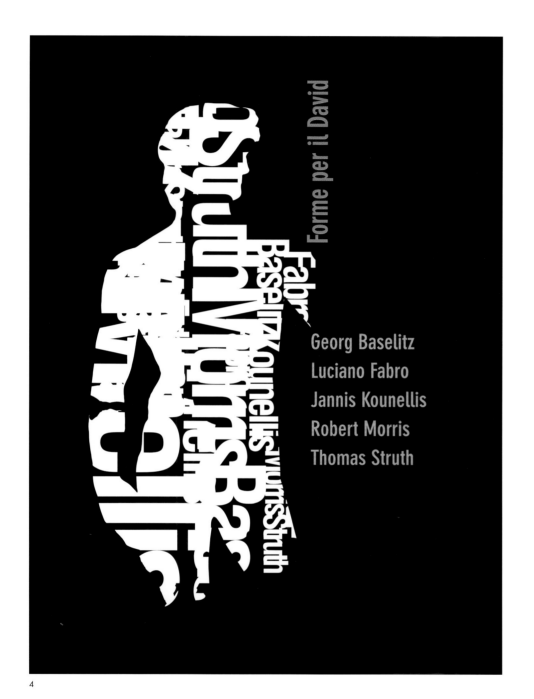

Forme per il David

Georg Baselitz
Luciano Fabro
Jannis Kounellis
Robert Morris
Thomas Struth

4

UNIVERSITÀ
DEL CAFFÈ
DI TRIESTE

5

Verónica Majluf

Armando Andrade

studioa
design and marketing consultancy

studioa
design and marketing consultancy

**a company associated to the
international design partnership**
www.idpweb.com

av salaverry 3328 lima 17 perú
t 264 2886 264 2887 264 2888 **f** 264 2891
e studioa@studioa.com.pe

Multidisciplinary company of design ...
Studioa is a multidisciplinary consulting company specialized in marketing, design and development of corporate strategies, constituted by a staff of professionals with expertise in a variety of areas and more than 25 years of experience in local and international markets.

The best of global and local market ...
We are members of IDP, (International Design Partnership), a worldwide network with offices in 14 countries, which provide us with great expertise in different disciplines of design and visual communication, with broad access to information, trends and a multicultural vision of worldwide and local projects aimed at international markets.

Design for added value ...
We understand design as a way to add value. Our task is helping our clients to achieve a better management of their existing assets with progressive solutions in the development of systems that meet the markets requirements.

1

5

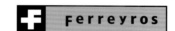

9

2

6

10

3

7

alicorp

11

4

centura
sab

8

Interbank

12

1 InVita
Life Insurance

2 Aquilo
Jewellery

3 Clínica San Felipe
Clinic

4 Marcelo Martire
Furniture

5 Miski
Agribusiness

6 Ferreyros
Machinery and Trucks

7 MALI «Museo de Arte de Lima»
Museum

8 Centura SAB
Private Banking

9 CRP «Corporación Radial del Perú»
Radio Corporation

10 Blubank
Bank

11 Alicorp
Food's Company

12 Interbank
Bank

1

2

3

a

4

La recuperación de la memoria

El primer siglo de la fotografía PERÚ 1842 - 1942

15 de noviembre 2001 - 17 de febrero 2002 MUSEO DE ARTE DE LIMA

5

The project encompasses the creation of the exhibit's verbal identity «The Recovery of Memory, 100 Years of Photography in Perú», the visual development, the pieces, the book design and the curator's advisory. The objective was to introduce a contemporary language that would contrast with the exhibit's concept of history and age. Its symbol is the synthesis of a photographic plate profile, which is used in several of the exhibit's platforms and which can be perfectly adapted to space requirements or graphic pieces.

1 Exhibition's Tickets

2 Poster

3 Invitation Card

4 Book

5 Museography

2

3

4

5

«The journey has begun» This is the airline's tangible promise of a new way of traveling, full of excitement and a young outlook. The well differentiated name "Magenta" embodies a unique experience that appeals to youthful and adventurous spirits. Its identity and visual system inspired by the pantone color chip takes possesion of contemporary Peruvian patterns where the magenta and yellow colors become the great axis of the visual comunication.

1 Luggage Tag

2 Seats

3 Boarding Pass

4 Business Cards

5 Travel Tickets

6 Airplane

7 Table Mat

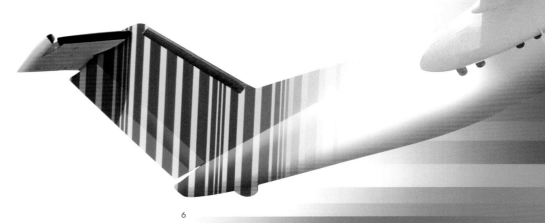

6

7

MAGENTA® **AIR**

Maarten Rijnen (The Netherlands)

1   Heineken
    Logo design 'Angel'
    Wieckse Witte - White beer

SAVE OUR CLIMATE

WWF, Greenpeace, VROM, UNEP
International Climate Symbol
Save our climate

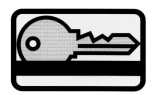

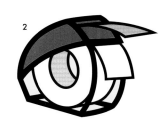
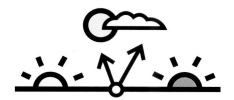

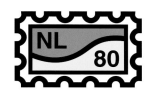

1 CPNB
Logo
Children's Book Week

2 TPG Post
Icons
Bussines Post

Bols Nederland
Icons
Bootz Liquer Brand

Maarten Rijnen (The Netherlands)

www.maartenrijnen.nl & www.mirandesign.nl

Ministerie van Verkeer en Waterstaat NL
Co-production: www.mirandesign.nl
Icon/Character Promoting use of Seatbelts - Armadillo

112

1.

2.

3.

4.

GeoCapital

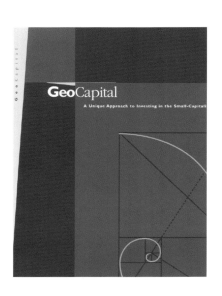

1. 1. Fidelis
2. Healthcare Services
3. Symbol / Advertising + Promotion

2. 1. AALDEF
2. Asian Pride Event
3. Exhibit Display and Advertising

3. 1. Unity Technology
2. Telecommunications Company
3. Print, Internet Marketing

4. 1. GeoCapital
2. Financial Services Firm
3. Print, Financial Services Promotion

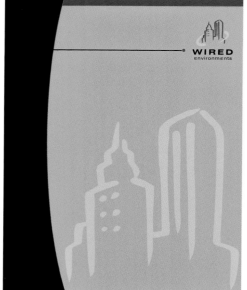

WIRED
environments

5. 1. Wired Environments
2. Urban computer networking
3. Print and Digital Collateral

6. 1. DuPont
2. ProCycling Championships
3. Event and Race Marketing

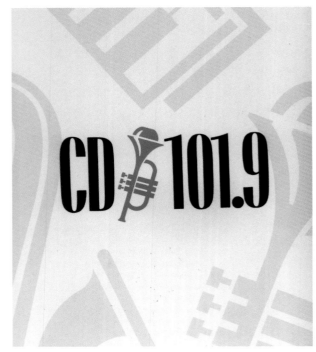

7. 1. WQCD/CD101.9 FM
2. Jazz Radio Station
3. Print and Digital Collateral

MINTERS
FUN FOOD & DRINK
menu

8. 1. Minters Restaurants
2. Bakery & Restaurant
3. Print and Digital Collateral

MINTERS

9. 1. City Valet
   2. Limousine and Car Service
   3. Advertising and Internet Promotion

10. 1. Tefefix
    2. Telephone Communications
    3. Print and Digital Collateral

11. 1. Orderin.com
    2. Restaurant Delivery Service
    3. Print, Advertising & Digital Collateral

WATERFRONT
MONTESSORI

12. 1. Waterfront Montessori
    2. Preschool
    3. Print and Digital Collateral

13. 1. Muze
    2. Music Information Retrieval
    3. Print and Digital Collateral

NEW YORK
NUMBERS

14. 1. NY State Lottery
    2. Numbers Game of Chance
    3. Print and Digital Collateral

15. 1. NY State Lottery
    2. Keno Game of Chance
    3. Print and Digital Collateral

16. 1. NY State Lottery Game
    2. Game of Chance
    3. Print and Digital Collateral

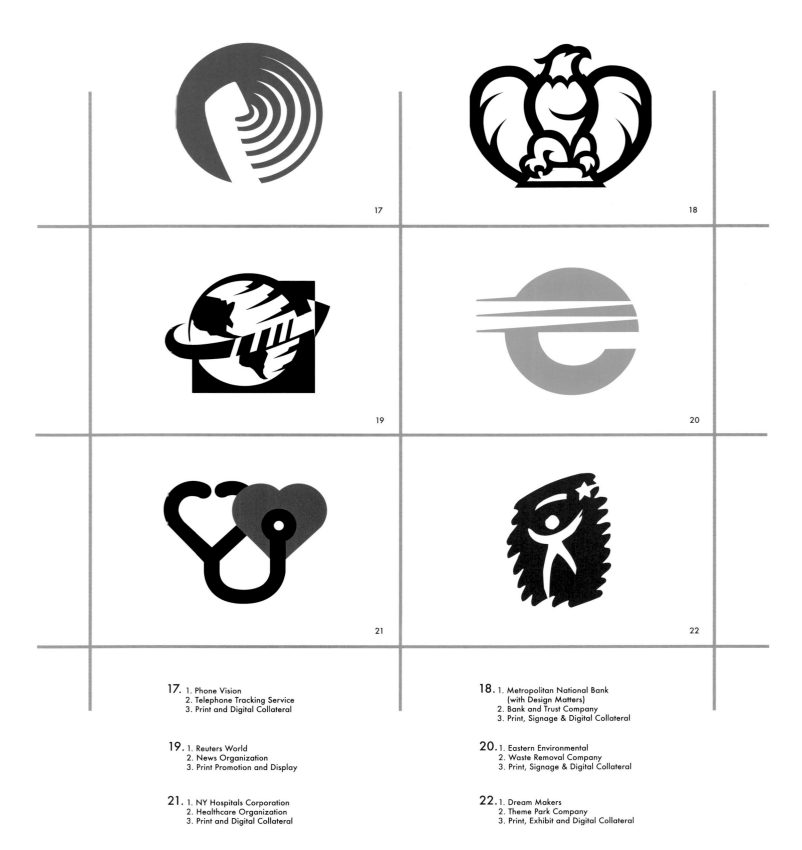

17

18

19

20

21

22

17. 1. Phone Vision
2. Telephone Tracking Service
3. Print and Digital Collateral

18. 1. Metropolitan National Bank
(with Design Matters)
2. Bank and Trust Company
3. Print, Signage & Digital Collateral

19. 1. Reuters World
2. News Organization
3. Print Promotion and Display

20. 1. Eastern Environmental
2. Waste Removal Company
3. Print, Signage & Digital Collateral

21. 1. NY Hospitals Corporation
2. Healthcare Organization
3. Print and Digital Collateral

22. 1. Dream Makers
2. Theme Park Company
3. Print, Exhibit and Digital Collateral

23

24

25

26

NATIONAL
DO NOT CALL
REGISTRY

23. 1. Perdido Productions
2. Airline Identity/Motion Picture
3. Print and Environmental

24. 1. Estee Lauder/Aveda
2. Health & Beauty
3. Print and Packaging Usage

25. 1. FTD (with G2)
2. Floral Delivery Service
3. Print, Web Advertising

26. 1. Federal Trade Commission
(with JDG Communications)
2. National 'Do Not Call' Registry
3. Print and Digital Collateral

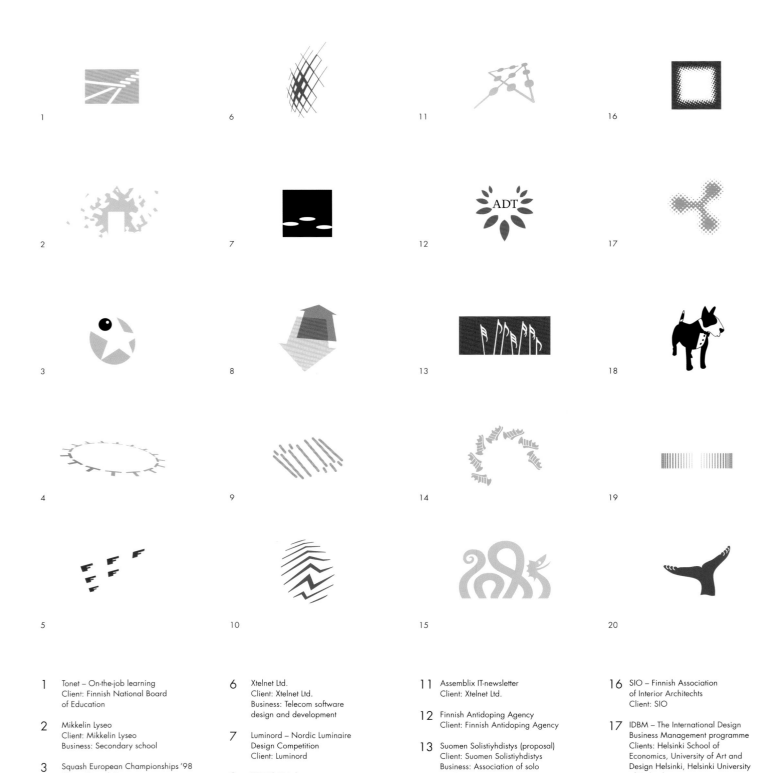

1   Tonet – On-the-job learning
    Client: Finnish National Board
    of Education

2   Mikkelin Lyseo
    Client: Mikkelin Lyseo
    Business: Secondary school

3   Squash European Championships '98
    Client: Squash European
    Championships '98

4   TTT – Finnish Association of Technical
    and Information Employees
    Client: TTT

5   Finavitec Ltd. (proposal)
    Client: Finavitec Ltd.
    Business: Aircraft manufacturer

6   Xtelnet Ltd.
    Client: Xtelnet Ltd.
    Business: Telecom software
    design and development

7   Luminord – Nordic Luminaire
    Design Competition
    Client: Luminord

8   PTM-Yhtiö Ltd.
    Client: PTM-Yhtiö Ltd.
    Business: Real estate agent

9   Strawbius Systems Ltd.
    Client: Strawbius Systems Ltd.
    Business: Refinement of
    recyclable raw materials

10 Aplac Solutions Corp.
    Client: Aplac Solutions Corp.
    Business: Develops and markets
    software for analog and RF designers

11 Assemblix IT-newsletter
    Client: Xtelnet Ltd.

12 Finnish Antidoping Agency
    Client: Finnish Antidoping Agency

13 Suomen Solistiyhdistys (proposal)
    Client: Suomen Solistiyhdistys
    Business: Association of solo
    musicians

14 Espoo Football Academy
    Client: Espoo Football Academy

15 Serena Water Amusement
    Park (proposal)
    Client: Blue inc.

16 SIO – Finnish Association
    of Interior Architechts
    Client: SIO

17 IDBM – The International Design
    Business Management programme
    Clients: Helsinki School of
    Economics, University of Art and
    Design Helsinki, Helsinki University
    of Technology

18 Suomen Solistiyhdistys (proposal)
    Client: Suomen Solistiyhdistys
    Business: Association of solo musicians

19 Muotoilutoimisto 360 astetta
    Client: Muotoilutoimisto 360 astetta
    Business: Design firm

20 Serena Water Amusement
    Park (proposal)
    Client: Blue inc.

21

22

23

24

25

26

27

30

28

31

29

32

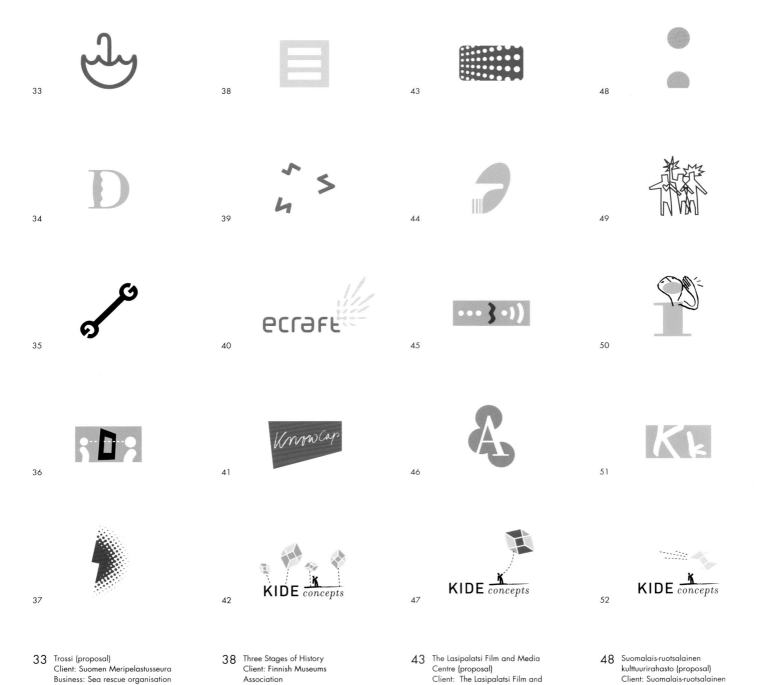

Marcelo Sapoznik «Experto en Marcas» (Argentina)

Marcelo is a Graphic and Advertising Design graduate from the Pan-American School of Art. He has a chair at the University of Buenos Aires in the Graphic Design school, and has taught and given lectures at several national universities. Marcelo has been a judge in numerous design and advertising competitions. His work has been featured in books published in Argentina, Brazil, USA, and Japan.

He is a founding member of Brandgroup | IDP (International Design Partnership). Marcelo has been a partner and project leader in the strategic development and implementation process of identities of the most recognized design companies in Argentina. In the last few years Marcelo has specialized in Brand Strategy and Identity Design development.

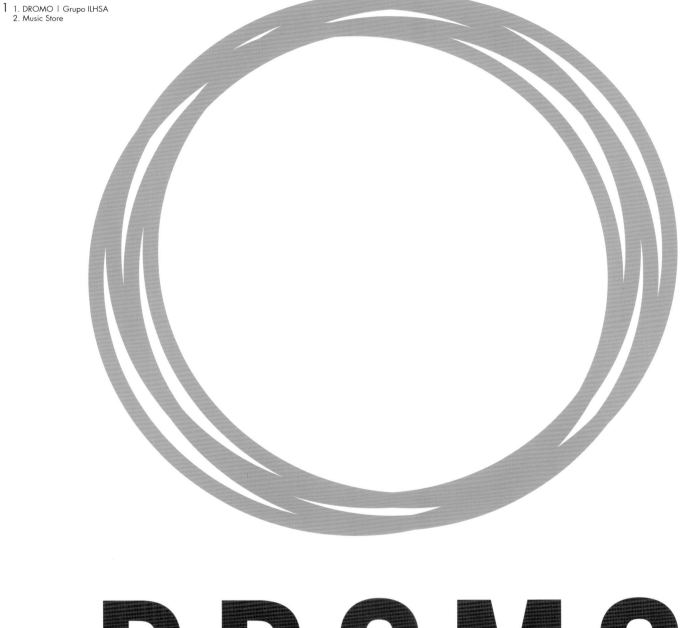

DROMO

Marcelo Sapoznik «Experto en Marcas» (Argentina)

2 1. OKKO
2. Departament Store
3. In collaboration with Carlos Venancio

3 1. Supermercados Disco
2. Supermarket
3. Developed at Fontana FVS

4 1. Telecom
2. Telecomunications
3. Developed at Fontana FVS

5 1. Fullzero | Ciudad Internet
2. Internet Service Provider
3. Developed at Brandgroup

6 1. Bansud
2. Bank
3. Developed at Fontana FVS

2

3

4

5

www.fullzero.com

6

3

7

8

9

10

11

12

Marcelo Sapoznik «Experto en Marcas» (Argentina)

13 1. Grupo ASSA
2. Technology
3. Developed at Brandgroup

14 1. Movicom Bellsouth
2. Telecommunication
3. Developed at Brandgroup

13

1.

2.

3.

1. White Plains Public Library (WPPL)
   Logo
   Looking to modernize its image, the new WPPL identity speaks to the sophisticated nature of this community resource and expresses their transition from solely books to an ever-increasing digital and online component in their offerings.

2. White Plains Public Library
   Color Palette

3. White Plains Public Library
   Library Card

4. White Plains Public Library (WPPL)
   Ads
   Located at the local commuter railroad station, these advertisements raise awareness to everyday issues that can be solved by the online services the WPPL provides. The comic book and pop art derived illustrations are both attention-getting, sophisticated and modern, reflecting the newly re-branded library.

4.

Pisarkiewicz Mazur & Co (USA)

1.

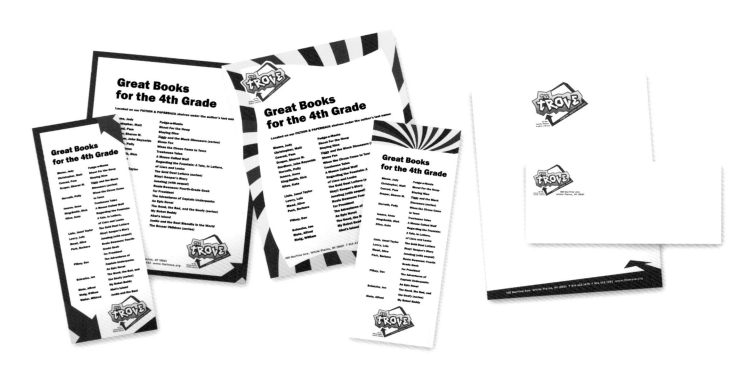

2.

3.

1. The Trove
   Logo
   We developed the name "The Trove"–
   a collection of valuable items discovered
   or found – for a new children's library
   facility for the White Plains Public Library,
   New York.

2. The Trove
   Color Palette
   A remarkable resource to its community,
   the library now needed to compete with
   other venues & entertainment vehicles for
   the attention of the children they served.
   We developed an identity that would
   appeal to the youth of today, targeting
   10 to 12 year olds.

3. The Trove
   Stationery and templates

4. The Trove
   Entryway design
   We set out to give this place a history
   and a real feeling of wonder and
   exploration. The design we created and
   the story of its discovery is now being
   realized.

5. The Trove
   The Map
   This map was designed to creatively
   express each of the various areas in The
   Trove. In naming each area, illustrations
   were done to enable the space designers
   to have an understanding of the attitude
   necessary to complete the brand's vision.

One sunny day in 2004, Louis and Andrea stopped by the library to see what intriguing new things they could discover. They did this almost every day, but on this particular day there was a special excitement in the air. Today the construction workers were coming to start building the new Children's Library.

For weeks the children had seen architects, engineers and librarians carrying blueprints that looked like treasure maps. Today at last, the workers put on their hard hats, picked up their sledgehammers and started to break through the wall.

The children joined a small crowd that watched from a distance as giant chunks of plaster and concrete crumbled away, bookshelves tumbled and clouds of dust filled the air. The haze cleared slowly, and streams of starry light poured through the opening to reveal a passageway beyond. The crowd gasped and pressed closer. A librarian stepped forward, with Louis and Andrea leading the way. The three held their breath and peered into the softly lit passage. In the distance they could see a wondrous place, filled with the promise of endless imagination, exploration and discovery.

"Its something amazing!" they called back to the waiting crowd. They didn't know it yet, but they had found The Trove, and their adventure was just beginning.

4.

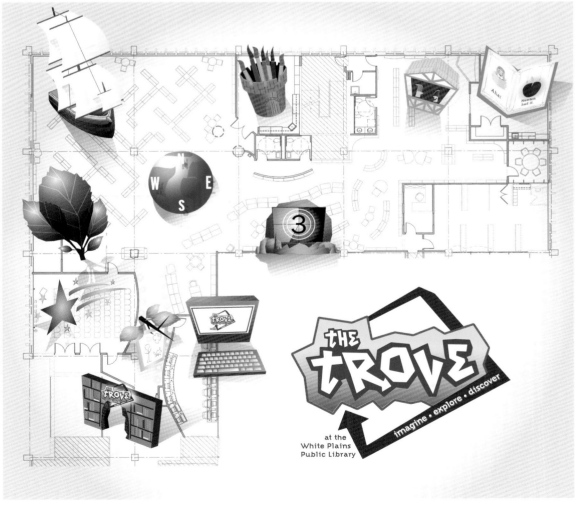

5.

1.

2.

3.

1. Shelterwood Financial Services LLC
   Logo
   A subsidiary of J.M. Huber Corporation, PM & Co created the name for the new business directly from their culture and business of timber management. The name draws from the system "shelter-wood" in which mature trees provide protection to the next generation.

2. Shelterwood Financial Services LLC
   Color Palette
   PM & Co created an identity that is both unique in this financial service sector and reflects the Huber natural resources background while also feeling very consumer friendly.

3. Shelterwood Financial Services LLC
   Marketing materials:
   Using heavy textured papers with embossing and vellum with clean elegant design, a rich expression of the Shelterwood metaphor was created to communicate a sense of connection and emotional attachment to this high net worth target.

4. Shelterwood Financial Services LLC
   Website
   The website was designed to provide important information to help visitors better understand the organization, its services and processes. The site is tied visually and verbally to all other communication materials.

4.

137

1 1.Compass
   2.Editorial Design

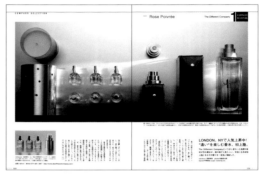

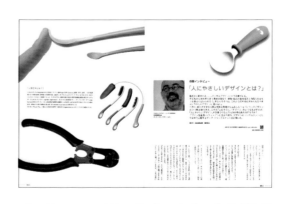

1

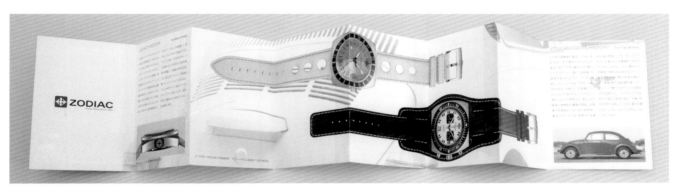

2

1   1.BroadBand Academy
     2.logo Mark

2   1.BroadBand Academy
     2.Pamphlet

3   1.Broadband Academy
     2.Business Card

4   1.Broadband Academy
     2.Mouse Pad

5   1.BroadBand Academy
     2.Envelope

1

2

3

4

5

6

7

 the Lemon Yellow, Inc.

The Lemon Yellow logo with its stylishly refreshing artistry is created by a single continuous brush stroke and has become our symbol of eternal creativity.

In 1979, Lemon Yellow stood out as the first and only design house in Taiwan. It has been the design company's goal and duty to provide clients with "tailor-made" service including product introduction, sales promotion, PR events, corporate identity system (CIS) and intergrated communication.

We and our clients have grown together by facing changes and challenges side by side for years. As a forerunner specializing in visual design, Lemony Yellow has helped to crate a new era for the industry by promoting the right image of the manufacturer's products to consumers.

Jack Pot Manufacturer Corp.
KG Telecom
Disaster Prevetion Research Center National Cheng Kung University
Zao-Kun Engineering Science & Technology Co., Ltd.

DESKNOTE

e Herber

DNC

Chai Found
Music Workshop

EVERYDAY ®

JUNIOR LAND

Elitegroup Computer systems Co.,Ltd.
DNC International Co.,Ltd.
Chai Found Music Workshop
Junior Land Co.,Ltd.

EHerber Enterprise Co.,Ltd.
Everyday Convenience Store Co., Ltd.
Tsai. Lee & Associates

National Percussion & Frame Drum Association
TAIWAN, R.O.C
Goodman Fieder International(Taiwan) Limited

Wangs' Tea
Wei Chuan Corp.

absolutreality
www.absolut.fr

1 Les Arts Décoratifs
Branding Identity Manual (80 pages) for a group of Museums (Paris-France)

GEMOLOGY ®

4 Gemology
Logotype and Packaging for a new range of Cosmetics

GEMOLOGY ®

Huile corps
Body oil

TOUS TYPES DE PEAUX

WOMEN'S FORUM ®
FOR THE ECONOMY & SOCIETY

5 Women's Forum For the Economy & Society
Branding Identity Manual

absolutreality
www.absolut.fr

6 Kiria
Branding Identity Manual and Interior Design
for a health-care concept-store

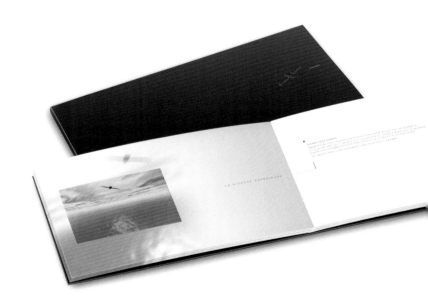

7 Eutelsat
Re-lifting of the Branding Identity
and print work (annual report, brochures, ...)

Tucker Design (Australia)

1.
1.	Cheviot Bridge
2.	Premium wine company identity and packaging

Welcome to the world of Tucker Design.

We'd like to introduce you to Tucker Design, our services and our work.

Our specialty and core business is graphic design – the field of communication graphics.

To us, graphic design is creating and communicating messages visually, finding the ideal solution through images, objects and environs. It's a blend of strategy, planning, knowledge, research and experience mixed together with creativity, passion and a touch of inspiration. In short, solving communication, marketing or business problems with effective, unique and memorable visual solutions.

Approaching 30 years of industry excellence, Tucker Design has earned the reputation as one of Australia's benchmark studios by consistently pushing the boundaries of what graphic design can encompass and achieve. Originally founded by Barrie Tucker and now led by eldest son Jody Tucker, Tucker Design is a multi-disciplined team of people whose collective aim is achieving positive and successful outcomes for our clients through creative excellence.

It's this type of dedication and expertise that has seen Tucker Design win a host of prestigious international design awards. While our client's satisfaction and success is our primary concern, it's always satisfying to be recognised by our peers.

We invite you to explore and discover Tucker Design's world for yourself.

Jody Tucker, Managing Director

Tucker Design Pty Ltd

Head Office & Studios
The Church Hall
6a George Street, Stepney
South Australia 5069

T +61 8 8362 4000
F +61 8 8362 3400

tuckers@tuckerdesign.com.au
www.tuckerdesign.com.au

Singapore Office
16 Upper Circular Road
Level 2 Benning House
Singapore 058414

T +65 9677 5024
F +65 6542 2682

lk7828@singnet.com.sg

2. 1. Powercell
   2. Battery cell brand

4. 1. Integra Plus
   2. Synthetic wine closure brand

5. 1. AP John Coopers
   2. Wine barrel makers
   3. Historical family company

3. 1. Tanunda Pines Golf Club
   2. Country golf club
   3. Golf course lined by pine trees in the world renowned
      wine region of Barossa Valley, Australia

2

3

4

5

6. 1. ASA Cork
   2. Natural wine cork company

7. 1. Matrix Integrated Holdings
   2. Hotel, Finance and
      Insurance companies

8. 1. ASA Cork
   2. Individual product brands

6

7

8

9. 1. Macaw Creek Winery
    2. Company identity and product brand

10. 1. Aquatas Tasmania
    2. Company identity
    3. Atlantic salmon and ocean trout product

11. 1. Boar's Rock
    2. Contract wine making company

12. 1. Willunga Basin Water Company
    2. Rural water purification plant

13. 1. Graetz Irrigation
    2. Rural irrigation specialists

MACAW CREEK

9

AQUATAS
TASMANIA

10

WILLUNGA BASIN
WATER COMPANY

12

Boar's Rock

11

GRAETZ
IRRIGATION

13

Tucker Design (Australia)

14. 1. Wendy's Supa Sundaes
    2. Ice cream and drinks
    3. International franchise

15

18

16

17

WAGNER, a global leader in the solar lamp and surface treatment sector was repositioned and all communication material for consumers, contractors and industry was redesigned. The goal was to create a clear, consistent communication, which is adequate for each target group. The SOLUTIONS industrial designers also translated the visual language into the product development. Additionally, the WAGNER GROUP was created, in which the 21 enterprises, 7 production plants and 14 international branches will be represented. For the purpose of entering new markets and distribution channels, SOLUTIONS developed the brand "premium class", including the entire brand communication and the product design of the solar lamps.

1

2

5

3

4

1	1. WAGNER	2	1. WAGNER	3	1. WAGNER	4	1. WAGNER	5	1. WAGNER
	2. Stationery		2. Contractor and industry brochures		2. Consumer brochures		2. W 550 fine spray system designed by SOLUTIONS		2. Poster

WAGNER GROUP

6

7

premium class

8

9

Vivanco, one of the leading suppliers of consumer electronics and computer accessories, wants to extend its competence in the innovative trend product sector for teenagers with "bazoo". The brand name, which was developed by SOLUTIONS, as well as the color trends and logo are aimed at teenagers of both sexes. The claim "bazoo – because yesterday is boring", supports the positioning of this brand.

3

2

1

4

5

6

Lecker is BioThek's leading natural food brand. In order to extend the positioning of this brand, a traditional yet modern concept was developed, which through the traditional woodcut illustrations reminds us, of how Grandma used to bake, while the colors are reminiscent of childrens books. This design has been transferred to brochures, pamphlets, packaging, baking utensils, recipe books, posters, displays, the internet and trade fair designs.

1

2

3

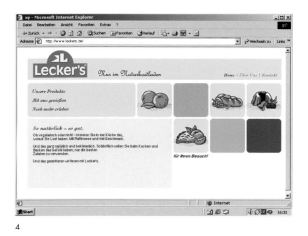

4

5

1   1. BioThek „Lecker's"
    2. Logo

2   1. BioThek „Lecker's"
    2. Brochure

3   1. BioThek „Lecker's"
    2. Packaging

4   1. BioThek „Lecker's"
    2. Website

5   1. BioThek „Lecker's"
    2. Trade fair

PUNICA a fruit juice brand belonging to the Sunny Delight Beverages Co. is aimed mainly at Children and teenagers. Originally, PUNICA produced just orange juice, but with the introduction of new tastes, the variety of products should communicate freshness and fun. The logo has been modernized and the so-called "PUNICA Oasis", which can be found in the entire above and below-the-line communication, was developed.

1

2

3

Brunazzi&Associati

Created in 1985 by Giovanni Brunazzi, one of the pioneers of company communication and corporate image in Italy, Brunazzi&Associati is one of a small number of Italian advertising agencies that specialise in corporate identity, publishing and packaging, which are able to provide exclusive, highly professional services in the field of integrated communication and image strategies.

Brunazzi&Associati coordinates its customers' various needs with specific and wide-ranging assistance, from industrial and product design to management of integrated communication projects, conventional advertising campaigns, the realisation of new package design solutions for brand products and private labels, the design of web sites, stands and promotional items, external relations and graphics projects for books, magazines, posters and quality publications.

As a result, every action plan studied by Brunazzi&Associati always depends on detailed examination of the customer company's existing image, accompanied by analysis of its manufacturing and distributional set-up, the competition and its reference market.

1

Brunazzi&Associati srl
Via Andorno 22,
10153 Torino Italy
tel. +39 01181 25 397
fax +39 01181 70 702
e-mail: info@brunazzi.com
www.brunazzi.com

3

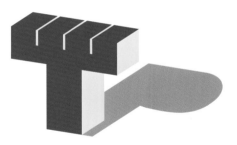

4

CITTA' DI TORINO

7

GFTNET
INTERNATIONAL NETWORK

FACIS

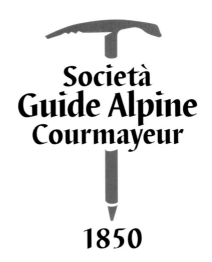

Società
Guide Alpine
Courmayeur

1850

10

11

Compagnie des Guides • Società Guide Alpine

1850
2000
Courmayeur

13

Arbiola®

15

12

14

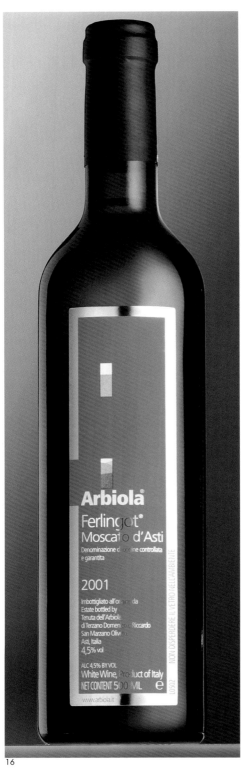

16

10 1. Società Guide Alpine Courmayeur
   2. Logo
   3. Mountaneering Guide

11/12 1. Info Mont Blanc
       2. Logo and sign
       3. Mountain weather Information Office

13/14 1. Società Guide Alpine Courmayeur
       2. Logo for Anniversary of 150 years
       3. The second oldest mountainering
          society in the world

15/16 1. Tenuta dell'Arbiola
       2. Logo, and wine labels
       3. Wine producer

17 1. Cinara
    2. Food industry Logo

18/19 1. Cinara
       2. Centrone brand Logo
       3. Logo and labels of vegetable in oil
          or in vinegar products

20 1. Monetti
    2. Melform Logo
    3. Equipment and solutions for the
       catering industries

21 1. Monetti
    2. Siberian Koala logo
    3. Logo deigned for a special product

22 1. Monetti
    2. Pelican Delicatesse logo
    3. Logo for a special product for aircraft
       catering

SUPERGA®

23

24

25

Maia
Costruzioni Edili

27

28

26

29

30

31

32

34

33

35

DAI (Switzerland)

www.dai.ch

dai is an agency specialized in creating brand architecture strategies that can be experienced

Naturalness, durability, simplicity. Guided by these key terms of reference, the team at dai (design, architecture, identification) – headed up by the agency's founder Florin Baeriswyl – developed a corporate identity for the new SZKB Asset Management. To give the bank's service offering and brand a tangible presence, dai prepared a comprehensive concept which in all its elements reflects the aspects of individual client service provided by the bank. dai also put this concept into practice for the interior design. Buildings and interiors express your company's philosophy and reinforce its identity. Architecture is experienced by employees and customers not only as an aesthetic but as an embodiment of your company's ethos and is part of branding.

dai developed the name, the logo, the corporate identity and the interior design, along with the advertising campaign for print and online media. A fully rounded identity, displaying a uniform quality in all its elements, was created by a single source.

www.dai.ch

相模湾の海の中を再現
「相模湾大水槽」
銀色にうねりながら泳ぐ
8,000匹のマイワシの群れは圧巻

クラゲの体内にいるような幻想的な癒し空間
「クラゲファンタジーホール」
常時約10種類のクラゲを展示

Minazo
Minamizouazarashi

Gomafuazarashi

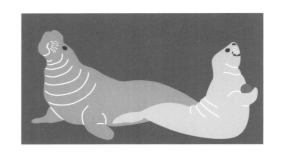

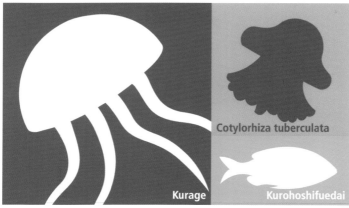

Midoriisoginchaku

Hondawara

Hatatatedai

Maiwashi

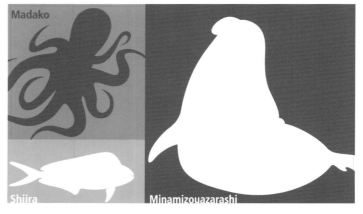

Hakofugu

Kouika

Takaashigani

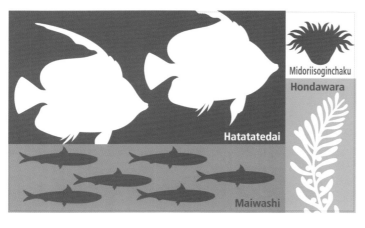

Kurage

Cotylorhiza tuberculata

Kurohoshifuedai

Madako

Shiira

Minamizouazarashi

Houbou

Dochizame

Umigame

Minokasago

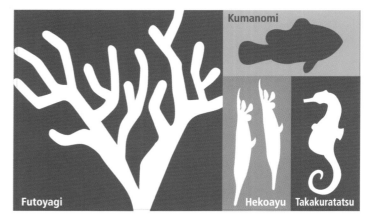

Kumanomi

Futoyagi

Hekoayu

Takakuratatsu

『新江ノ島水族館』では、国内外で活躍するアーティストとコラボレートするアーティストプロジェクト「enoshima aquarium ART WORKS」を始動。第 1 回目として、漫画家、イラストレーター、写真家など、6 名のアーティストが参加し、「海の動物たち」や「湘南」をテーマにオリジナルアートを制作しました。

【参加アーティスト と主なオリジナルグッズ】
玖保キリコ（漫画家）	チョコレートクランチ缶（楕円缶）
プレイセッツプロダクツ（イラストレーター）	チョコレートクランチ缶（四角缶）
森井ユカ（立体粘土作家）	ドロップ缶
エド・エンバリー（絵本作家）	ドロップ缶
広田行正（写真家）	A5 版ノート
松田崇志（イラストレーター）	A5 版ノート

新江ノ島水族館　〒251-0035 神奈川県藤沢市片瀬海岸 2-19-1　TEL 0466-29-9960
http://www.enosui.com

1

1   1. Client name Treasury Box
      2.Theme of Design Guaranty and package

2   1. Client name Treasury Box
      2. Theme of Design Name Card

3   1. Client name Treasury Box
      2. Theme of Design Catalog

4   1. Client name Treasury Box
      2. Theme of Design Catalog and guaranty

2

3

4

1

2

3

4

5

6

7

8

9

1 Client Name:
Taitung Farmer's Associations
Journey to the East Supply
Center

2 Client Name:
Twin Oak Garden

3 Client Name:
Tessmay

4 Client Name:
Ever Prosperous Int'l Co., Ltd.

5 Client Name:
China External Trade
Development Council

6 Client Name:
Chunghwa Telecom

7 Client Name:
THum Chen Trading Co., Ltd.

8 Client Name:
Peace Square

9 Client Name:
V-touch Network Restaurant

1

2

3

4

5

6

7

8

1   Client Name:
    Taiwan Graphic Design
    Association

2   Client Name:
    Sea Gaia

3   Client Name:
    Flamingo

4   Client Name:
    Guilin Merryland

5   Client Name:
    O-lliance

6   Client Name:
    New Woman Magazine

7   Client Name:
    Galerie Elegance Taipei

8   Client Name:
    Stony Image

1

2

3

4

5

6

7

8

9

1 Client Name:
Powerrock Interior Design
Company

2 Client Name:
Journey to the East

3 Client Name:
Council of Agriculture
Executive Yuan

4 Client Name:
Zhong Cai Ren Jia

5 Client Name:
Feng Crystal

6 Client Name:
Green Ferns

7 Client Name:
Taiwan Floriculture Exports
Association (TFEA)

8 Client Name:
Council of Agriculture
Executive Yuan

9 Client Name:
Bai Li Tou Hong

1

2

3

4

5

6

7

8

9

1   Client Name:
    Foundation of Taiwan Industry
    Service

2   Client Name:
    Philips Personal Computers

3   Client Name:
    Time Holder Mask

4   Client Name:
    D&S

5   Client Name:
    National Archives Administration

6   Client Name:
    Ren-Ai Township Office

7   Client Name:
    American Polylite

8   Client Name:
    Industrial Development Bureau,
    Ministry of Economic Affairs

9   Client Name:
    Green Garden

1. Sydney Olympic Park Authority (AUS)
   Kids in the Park
   Identity and brand implementation

2

3

4

5

6

7

Over the last 20 years Ezio Bocci has developed a global communication approach fully in line with its clients' marketing strategies.

The team takes an active part in the development of the client's marketing communication strategy, which it translates into incisive messages and images.

A global approach maintains the visual harmony of the set of communication products deployed to implement the strategy. It becomes a strike force that makes it possible to attain targets more quickly, since everything converges in the same direction for both image and message.

In many business partnerships the Ezio Bocci Immagine & Comunicazione teams helps its clients to get the best out of their marketing strategy, contributing solutions that confer a unique value on a product or enterprise so that it can make its mark in the market.

Via delle fratte, 51
00044 Frascati (Rome)
ITALY

phone : ++39 06 94 22 062
info@eziobocci.com
www.eziobocci.com

contact: Sylvie Gagnon

1. 1. Client : Hotel Barocco
   2. Country : Italy
   3. Category : hotel
   4. Production Date: 2001

2. 1. Client : Salumificio Castelli S.p.A.
   2. Country : Italy
   3. Category : food
   4. Production Date: 2002

3. 1. Client : Salumificio Castelli S.p.A.
   2. Country : Italy
   3. Category : food
   4. Production Date: 2002

4. 1. Client : Kao Corporation
   (collaboration with Kao Design Department)
   2. Country : Japan
   3. Category : chemical products
   4. Production Date: 2001

5

6

KNOWLEDGE FOR BUSINESS

7

SUPERCOM
strategie d'impresa

8

9

10

5 1. Client : Chef's Choice Ltd
   2. Country : Malta
   3. Category : food
   4. Production Date: 2003

8 1. Client : Supercom s.r.l.
   2. Country : Italy
   3. Category : marketing
   4. Production Date: 2002

6 1. Client : Industria Mancini Olearia S.p.A.
   2. Country : Italy
   3. Category : food
   4. Production Date: 1998

9 1. Client : Ciao Italia
   2. Country : Italy
   3. Category : import-export
   4. Production Date: 2001

7 1. Client : Pegaso Uno s.r.l.
   2. Country : Italy
   3. Category : web site
   4. Production Date: 2002

10 1. Client : Trillostore
    2. Country : Italy
    3. Category : store
    4. Production Date: 2002

expert*i*talia
travel & events

11

12

-FIORI del BENE

13

14

FESTIVAL DELLE VILLE TUSCOLANE

15

16

11 1. Client : Expertitalia s.r.l.
    2. Country : Italy
    3. Category : tourism
    4. Production Date: 2003

12 1. Client : Met Sviluppo S.p.A.
    2. Country : Italy
    3. Category : information technology
    4. Production Date: 2004

13 1. Client : I Fiori del Bene
    2. Country : Italy
    3. Category : publisher
    4. Production Date: 2004

14 1. Client : municipality of Frascati
    2. Country : Italy
    3. Category : public library
    4. Production Date: 2004

15 1. Client : municipality of Frascati
    2. Country : Italy
    3. Category : show business
    4. Production Date: 1994

16 1. Client : Sipleda S.p.A.
    2. Country : Italy
    3. Category : publisher
    4. Production Date: 2001

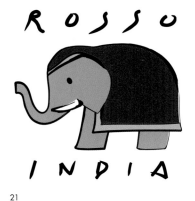

17 1. Client : Bricostore s.r.l.
    2. Country : Italy
    3. Category : Supermarket
    4. Production Date: 2002

18 1. Client : Elmax s.r.l.
    2. Country : Italy
    3. Category : mechanical equipment
    4. Production Date: 2000

19 1. Client : municipality of Frascati
    2. Country : Italy
    3. Category : museum
    4. Production Date: 2001

20 1. Client : Ron Sachs Communication
    2. Country : USA
    3. Category : web site
    4. Production Date: 2003

21 1. Client : Rosso India
    2. Country : Italy
    3. Category : clothing
    4. Production Date: 2004

社会福祉法人聖ヨハネ会

桜町病院
SAKURAMACHI HOSPITAL

1

3

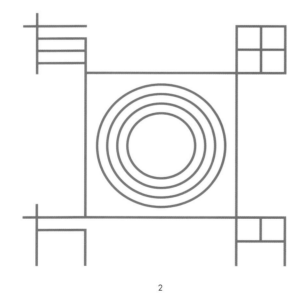

2

WORLD GOOD DESIGN

4

1 1. Sakuramachi Hospital　　**2** 1. D hand A　　**3** 1. New National Theatre, Tokyo　　**4** 1. World Good Design
2. Brand of Arita Ceramic　　　　2. NNT Dorama Studio　　　　2. Design Consultant
　　(ARITA-HOUEN)

5

戦争と万博

6

7

Amenity Design

8

5-6 1. Bijutsu Shuppan-Sha, Ltd
2. Event Poster / Title of Book

7 1. Villa Prana Shanti
2. Community

8 1. Amenity Design
2. Gallery

DESIGN QUEST

9

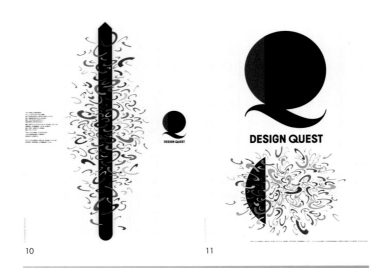

10

11

12

13

CINEWORK

14

15

9-11 1. DESIGN QUEST
2. Design Exhibition

12-13 1. PABLO WORK SHOP
2. Music Studio

14-15 1. CINE WORK Co.,Ltd.
2. Audio Visual Production

16

17

18

19

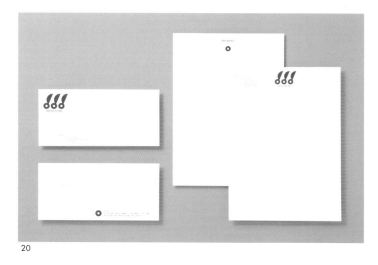

20

21

16-17 1. ST.JOHN'S HOSPICE

18-19 1. Wakana Co.,Ltd.
       2. Food company

20-21 1. Dai Nippon Printing Co.,Ltd.
       2. Design Gallery

NIME

22

EASY EDIT NIME

25

28

MATIERE

23

ALICE

26

29

VISUAL MESSAGE

24

27

DAPHNIA

30

22 1. National Institute of
      Multimedia Education
    2. University

23 1. MATIERE
    2. Fashion Studio

24 1. VISUAL MESSAGE
    2. Publisher

25 1. National Institute of
      Multimedia Education
    2. Teaching Material

26 1. Association on Living for
      Ideal Care Enhanced
    2. Society for Study of Medical

27 1. Sagacho Exhibit Space
    2. MUSES (Music at Sagacho Exhibit Space)

28 1. Cipta Budaya Bali Foundation
      Japan Office

29 1. Fujisetsu Co.,Ltd.
    2. Machine Design

30 1. DAPHNIA
    2. Music Production

ShoEi

31

34

中央歯科クリニック

37

DOK

32

摘 星 館

35

38

IBUKI
PLANNING OFFICE

33

靜

36

39

---

31 1. Shoei Foods Co., Ltd.
    2. Food company

32 1. Uwajima Contemporary Art
    2. Art Publishing

33 1. IBUKI PLANNING OFFICE
    2. Display Production

34 1. PABLO WORK SHOP
    2. Title of CD (KOE : VOICE)

35 1. Tekiseikan
    2. Gallery

36 1. F.C. Seiwa
    2. Japanese-Style Confectionery (SHIZUKA)

37 1. Chuo Dental Clinic

38 1. Cosmo P.R. Co., Ltd.
    2. Medical Technology

39 1. Yoshida Dental Clinic

hue.*visualab* | sdn bhd

www.huevisualab.com

Company
Hue Visualab Sdn Bhd

Project description
A contemporary set of communication materials was produced for Hue Visualab, a broadcast design and web development company. Designed on the concept of "Paintings in motion" these materials were to present creativity, professionalism and uniqueness. Boldness against normality, the dreamlike butterfly motions 'change' and the logotype seamlessly blends modern with old calligraphy fonts for a unique twist.

1 ATTHA HOLDINGS

2 JUROBUILDERS
STEEL AT ITS BEST

3 NUETEL

4 QUADSOLUTIONS
There is always a way.

5 AXISWARE.NET
TECHNOLOGIES

6 BrandAttic

7

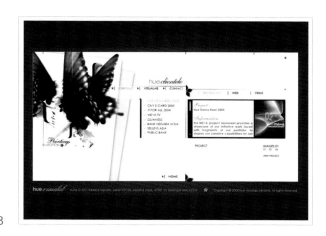

8

TEAM CREATIF (France & Brazil)

Philosophy

"Let's be partners in success"

"Let's be partners in success" is the expression of our passion, our everyday engagement towards our clients, their brands and their products.

Our N°1 objective is being at the service of our clients to respond efficiently to their objectives.
This demands great creativity and strong reactivity, a sharp understanding of consummers and the markets explored, pertinance and performance from our strategic recommandations.

Here lies the secret behind the loyalty of our clients, and the success of their... "our" brands and products, whether on a local or on an international basis.

We have worked for "local markets" in 48 countries!

Managers
Nick CRAIG: President
Sylvia VITALE ROTTA: Managing Director
Date of creation: 1986
Personnel: 102
Agencies Worldwide: Paris, São Paolo

Aeras of Expertise
Brand and Packaging Design / Product Design / Brand, Corporate and Service Design / Brandname creation / Sales Publishing / Environement Design / POS / Merchandising / Theatralisation.

Clients
Food sector
Bongrain / Cadbury-Schweppes / Campbell / Danone Group Worldwide / Georgia Pacific / Intersnack / Mars Group Worldwide / Merisant / New Zealand Milk / Reckitt Benckiser / Sadia (Brazil) / Sara Lee.

Corporate
AFME / Danone / Damart / Evian Masters / France Galop / Ligue de Football Professionnel / Masterfoods.

Other Sectors
Bic Shavers / Charles Christ / Nathan / Vivendi Universal.

TEAM CREATIF PARIS
89, rue de Miromesnil
Tel.: 01 42 89 90 00
Fax: 01 42 89 90 01
E-mail: team@team-creatif.com
Web: http://www.team-creatif.com

TEAM CREATIF SAO PAOLO
Avenida São Gabriel 201-CJ804
Jardim Paulista Sao Paulo Brazil
CEP: 01 435 001
Tel: 00 55 11 37 04 62 48
Fax: 00 55 11 30 71 07 59

Team Créatif:
*Elected "Design Agency of the year"
in 2001.*

Sadia Group 7.
*Strategic Visual Audit, Brand and Packaging Identity /
Brazil and Middle East*

New Zealand Milk 8.
Global Brand and Packaging Identity / Worldwide

Ligue de Football Professionnel 9.
Visual Identity / Corporate applications / France

Mars Group 10.
Corporate Identity of the group and applications / Worldwide

Mars Group 1.

Brand implementation Worldwide
Strategic audit / Creation of Brand and
Packaging Identity

Danone Group 2.

Creation of Brand and
Packaging Identity / Worldwide

Vivendi Universal 3.

Creation of Packaging Identity /
Branded Colour

Danone Group 4.

Brand implementation Worldwide
Strategic audit / Creation of the
Danone Corporate Identity /
Brand and Packaging Identity /
Special events Worldwide

Merisant Group 5.

Lifting of the Brand and
Packaging Identity / Worldwide

Sara Lee Group 6.

Creation of Brand and
Packaging Identity / France

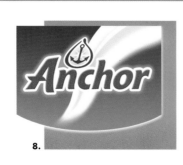

7. 8. 9. 10.

Brandnew·design (The Netherlands)

Competitive Packaging Design®

COMPANY STATEMENT
We live and breathe brands and packaging design!

COMPETITIVE PACKAGING DESIGN®
Brandnew·design has chosen
to focus on packaging design.
Our ideas and activities
related to brands, propositions
and products, are all based
on 'competitiveness'.
Therefore we use term
Competitive Packaging Design®,
in which the everyday battle
on the shelf has a central place.
This requires a specific way of
working and also a certain
mentality, combined with
specialised knowledge of a broad
range of other related services.
These include 3D structural design,
New Product Development and
Brand World.

ADRESS
Brandnew·design
P.O.Box 289
1380 AG Weesp
The Netherlands

www.brandnew.nl

CONTACT
Robert Kuiper
E. robert.kuiper@brandnew.nl
T. +31 (0)294 492 149
F. +31 (0)294 415 163

1 Royal Friesland Foods
Project: Go!

Brand & Identity
development for a 0% fat
dairy brand with 100 %
taste.

2 United Biscuits
Project: Sultana

Brand & Identity
development for a healthy
in-between snacking brand.

3 Koningshoeven
Project: La Trappe

We chose for very "Trappist"
like style for the brand to
ensure heritage and
calmness.

4 Katja Fassin
Project: Katja

A strong iconic Brand
Identity building on the
name and recognition
of Cats.

5 Caulils
Project: Caulils

The creating of a look &
feel of ancient times in a
modern appearance.

6 UTO
Project: Joseph Guy

Development of a rich and
meaningful icon connecting
the brand with its origin
and ambition.

Brandnewdesign

IDENTITY Ltd. (Estonia)

Identity Ltd., ESTONIA
Designers: Ionel Lehari, Maret Põldre, Jaakko Matsalu, Kaarel Kivikangur, Andrei Giritš
Theme: Selection of symbols from 2002/2004

Identity Ltd., ESTONIA
Designers: Ionel Lehari, Maret Põldre
Client: LeoExpress Ltd.
Category: Web Design and Direct Marketing
Production Date: 2004
Theme: Corporate Identity

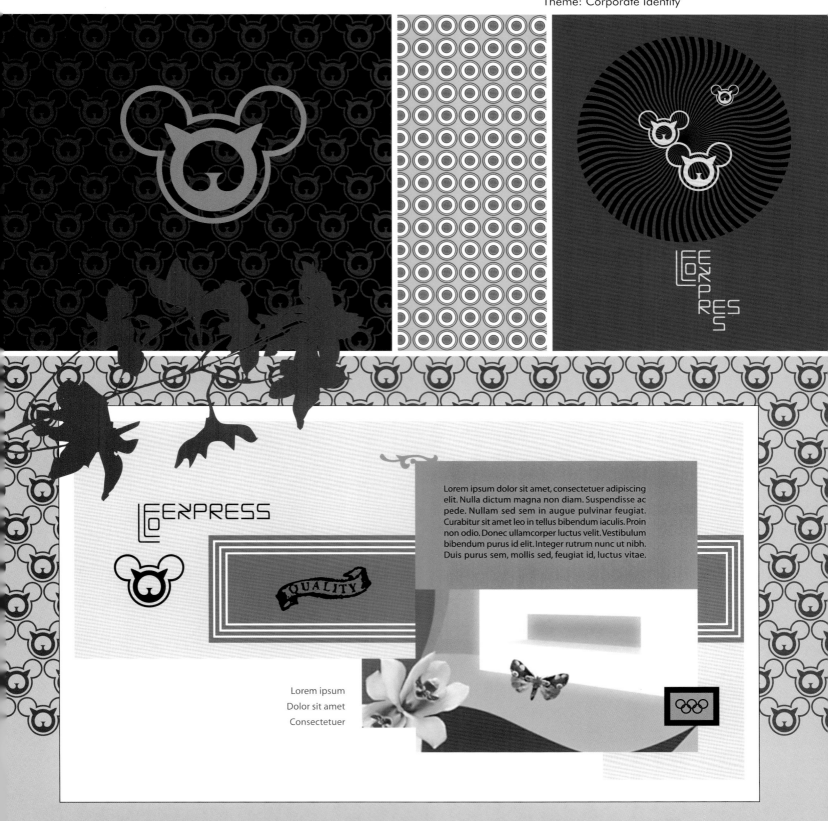

Lorem ipsum dolor sit amet, consectetuer adipiscing elit. Nulla dictum magna non diam. Suspendisse ac pede. Nullam sed sem in augue pulvinar feugiat. Curabitur sit amet leo in tellus bibendum iaculis. Proin non odio. Donec ullamcorper luctus velit. Vestibulum bibendum purus id elit. Integer rutrum nunc ut nibh. Duis purus sem, mollis sed, feugiat id, luctus vitae.

Lorem ipsum
Dolor sit amet
Consectetuer

IDENTITY Ltd. (Estonia)

Identity Ltd., ESTONIA
Designers: Ionel Lehari, Maret Põldre
Client: PopPartner Ltd.
Category: Point-of-Purchase
Production Date: 2004
Theme: Corporate Identity

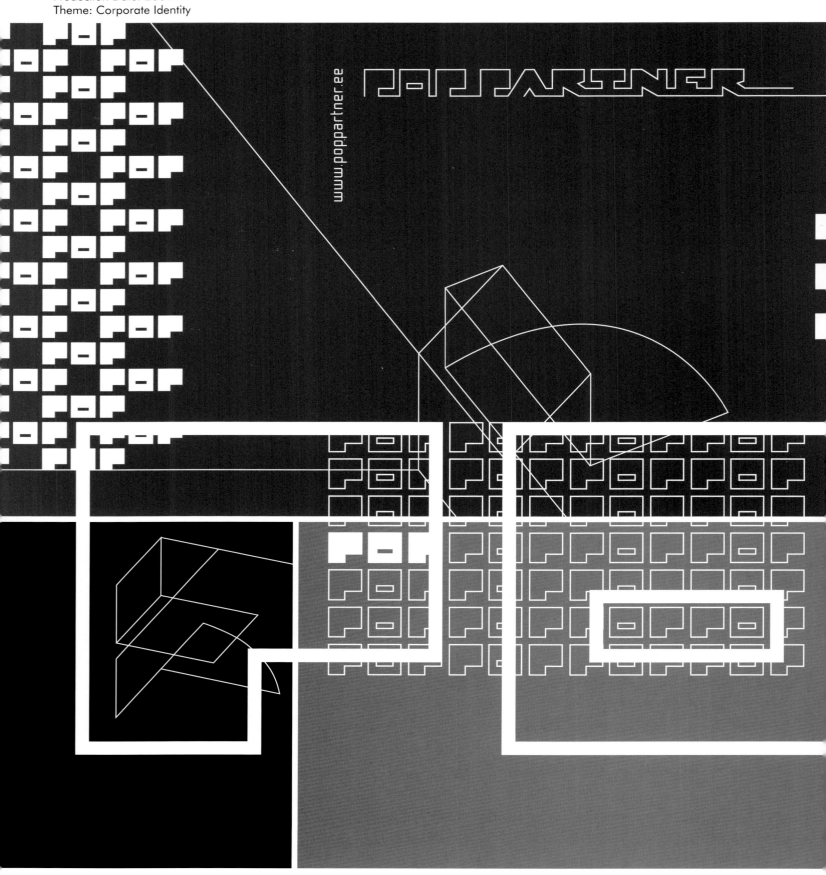

Identity Ltd., ESTONIA
Designer: Ionel Lehari, Maret Põldre
Client: Ideestuudio
Category: Photography
Production Date: 2003/2004
Theme: Corporate Identity

touched by mountain

touched by mountain

1
1. Fairworld Limited
2. Rainforest Organic Honey
3. Organic Brazilian Honey
4. Glass jar with plastic label
5. Money from sale of the product is donated to protect a selection of Amazonian endangered species.

2
1. Filter Clear Limited
2. Brand/Identity design
3. Deep bed filtration units
4. Various
5. The units use a filter of different sized stones to remove
particles in liquid/water. Logo represents the stones.

3
1. SNAP
2. Identity/Brand
3. Range of healthy food products
4. Various
5. A simple but strong logo designed to work across
food packaging, van livery, marketing material etc.

4
1. The Qibla Cola Company
2. New Qibla Cola can for Australia
3. Soft Drink Branding
4. Aluminium can
5. A very modern design moving the client away from their previous "Coca-Cola" feeling brand.

5
1. Albyn of Stonehaven
2. Sunsure
3. Sunburn detection lens
4. Pre-shaped clear plastic packaging
5. Brand, packaging form and product development
across three pricing levels of the product.

6
1. Venture Viewer
2. Brand/Identity design
3. Venture capital matchmaking company
4. Stationery, marketing material and website
5. The logo represents looking very closely at their venture requirements both client and recipient.

7
1. Expand Marketing Limited
2. Brand/Identity design
3. Marketing and product development company
4. Stationery, marketing material and website
5. This logo represents reaching higher goals - with our help.

8
1. Pinnacle Telecommunications plc
2. Brand/Identity design
3. Telecommunications company
4. All branded material and signage
5. Pinnacle Telecomms - the hub of a network of large, medium, small and mobile users

2

3

5

4

6

7

8

PROAD IMAGE DESIGN (Taiwan)

PROAD IMAGE DESIGN

Proad design is equal to a unique and fresh concept in design revolution. By combining diverse expertise in strategic design and focusing in furthering the progress of design with a professional and enthusiastic approach to problem solving, we, at Proad, have been able to deliver a powerful image to many Taiwan enterprises. Our packaging design expertise has proven essential in delivering a professional image to local businesses and our ability to offer a powerful visual store identity has also opened new horizons for many Taiwan O.B.M enterprises. Our clients range from computer communications and consumer electronic companies to chemical and material industries. We have been successful in working with customers first hand to insure on-brand development and translating a client's business vision into a visible expression of the company ensuring acceptance of such companies in the international market. Our innovative ideas, expertise, and strategic design can offer our clients "add on" values and provide them with increased revenues for their respective markets.

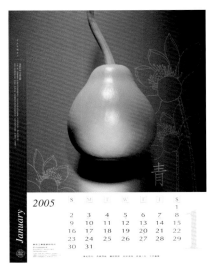

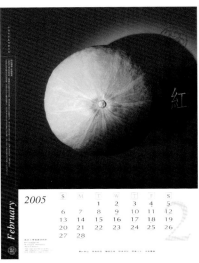

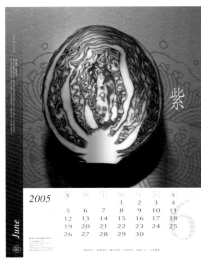

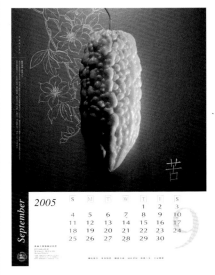

FOOD INDUSTRY RESEARCH AND DEVELOPMENT INSTITUTE (CALENDAR)

GREEN AIR HEALTH TECHNOLOGY

PROAD IMAGE DESIGN (Taiwan)

GIRAFFE ENGLISH

MILESTONES

BEING NUMBER ONE IS OUR GOAL

Pro Fortune Industry Co. Ltd. was established in 1987, having grown out of a previous company, Futing (FTC). Since its inception, Pro Fortune has dedicated itself to the supply of high quality products. It has vertically integrated its tooling production and expanded its product lines. As a result of competitiveness and successful performance in the market, Pro Fortune has developed auto parts molds and tools for OE vehicle makers such as Toyota, Honda, Nissan, Isuzu etc... The company's reliable engineering standards have also enabled it to make inroads into the competitive European market.

Our growth has been constant and steady, based on reinvestment of capital and sound financial policies. This has seen us develop a firm company base in Taipei, with warehousing facilities in the United States to support this important part of our market.

(Focus)

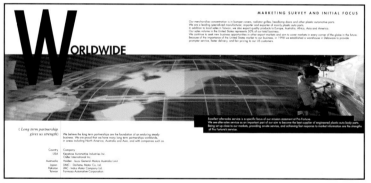

WORLDWIDE

MARKETING SURVEY AND INITIAL FOCUS

Our merchandise concentration is in bumper covers, radiator grilles, headlamp doors and other plastic automotive parts.
We are a leading specialized manufacturer, importer and exporter of mainly plastic auto parts.
In addition to local sales in Taiwan, we also export quality products to Europe, Australia, Africa, Asia and America.
Our sales volume in the United States represents 30% of our total business.
We continue to seek new business opportunities in other export markets and aim to cover markets in every corner of the globe in the future.
Because of the importance of the United States market to our business, in 1998 we established a warehouse in Delaware to provide prompter service, faster delivery, and fair pricing to our US customers.

Excellent after-sales service is a specific focus of our mission statement at Pro Fortune.
We see after-sales service as an important part of our aim to become the best supplier of engineered plastic auto body parts.
Being set up close to our markets, providing on-site service, and achieving fast response to market information are the strengths of Pro Fortune's service.

(Long term partnership gives us strength)

We believe the long term partnerships are the foundation of an enduring steady business. We are proud that we have many long term partnerships worldwide, in areas including North America, Australia and Asia, and with companies such as:

Country	Company
USA	Keystone Automotive Industries Inc.
	Order International Inc.
Australia	Holden - Isuzu General Motors Australia Limit
Japan	DMC - Daihatsu Motor Co. Ltd.
Pakistan	IMC - Indus Motor Company Ltd.
Taiwan	Formosa Automotive Corporation.

PEOPLE

(Human Resources)

Human resources are central to our success at Pro Fortune. We believe that to be a good employer, we must provide our employees with career opportunities and job satisfaction. Together with our employees, we can achieve our company goals.

We employ around 150 staff members, with a well-established administration department to support our engineering and manufacturing staff. On-job training is provided to enhance technical skills, and to ensure team cooperation and a pleasant working environment.

WE ARE A DETERMINED AND WELL-PREPARED PLAYER

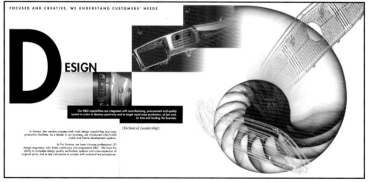

FOCUSED AND CREATIVE, WE UNDERSTAND CUSTOMERS' NEEDS

DESIGN

Our R&D capabilities are integrated with manufacturing, procurement and quality control in order to develop synchrony and to target rapid mass production, at low cost, on time and leading the business.

In Taiwan, few vendors possess both mold design capabilities and mass production facilities. As a leader in our business, we introduced CAD/CAM molds and fixture development systems.

At Pro Fortune, we have in-house professional 3D design engineers, who foster continuous and progressive R&D. We have the ability to complete design quality verification systems and cross-inspection of original parts, and to test instruments to comply with on-board test procedures.

(Technical Leadership)

WE AIM TO MEET OUR CUSTOMERS' CHALLENGES WITH TOTAL SOLUTIONS

We have positioned ourselves as a manufacturer which implements the latest technology in a vertically integrated process, in order to achieve economies of scale, mass production cost control and flexible production to reduce inventory risk.

Owing to our initial efforts to raise quality standards, improve our manufacturing processes, and develop better packaging designs, our products have been very well-received in the market. We are now one of Taiwan's major plastic manufacturers. Recent innovations have included a corporate image concept, new logo, and a vibrant and active new brand image which meets the spirit of challenge and innovation in the 21st century.

(Positioning)

SOLUTION

INFOMEDIA

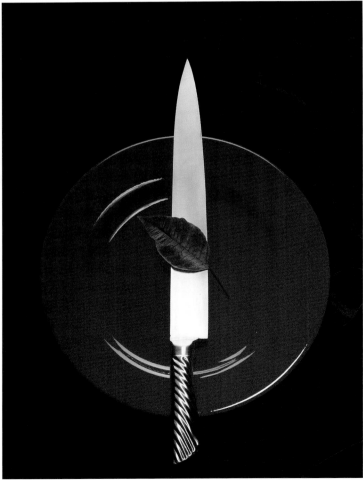

KING'S KNIFE

Creating A New Face
For Taiwan Design

為了讓台灣的設計與創意躍升國際舞台，台灣創意設計中心除了推動與國際設計組織進行策略統整與合作外，
也加強與國際知名設計組織如KIDP(Korean Institute of Design Promotion)、JDF(Japan Design Foundation)、
DDC(Dansk Design Center)以及APCI(Agency for the Promotion of Industrial Creation)進行聯繫交流
另外，台灣創意設計中心也積極推動國際設計資訊整合與人才培訓，重點推動工作包括，國際設計人才養成，
促成人才的海外進修：引進國際和名設計公司，促成國際交流、強化與全球設計資料庫的連結整合，
如美國的Core77、CMG、GF Plastic、日本的Axis、德國的Design Report⋯⋯等。
為提升台灣的創意研發能力，台灣創意設計中心也積極與國際學術研究單位進行基礎研究、
趨勢研究及應用技術研究，如感性工學、綠色設計、通用設計等，合作的對象包含日本的筑波、千葉大學、
美國的MIT Media Lab、德國的Essen 大學等。 創意，讓台灣看見世界；也讓世界看見台灣

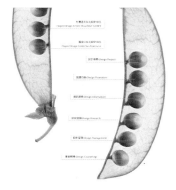

整合 創意設計的領導範疇

Numerous Multifaceted
Tasks Serving As One
Single Entity

審視 �旅能量及迎專業營運思維

A Successful Design
Reached By Thorough
Organization

｜推廣｜ 尋找設計的卓越價值

Leading The Way
To Extraordinary Value

｜轉載｜ 創造台灣產品設計新霸榮

Shaping The Future Of
Product Design

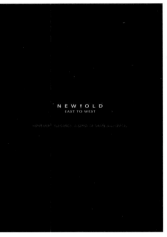

NEW OLD

RETEK

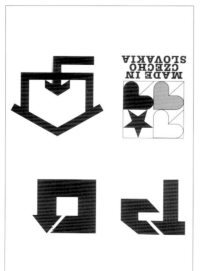

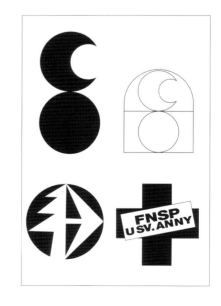

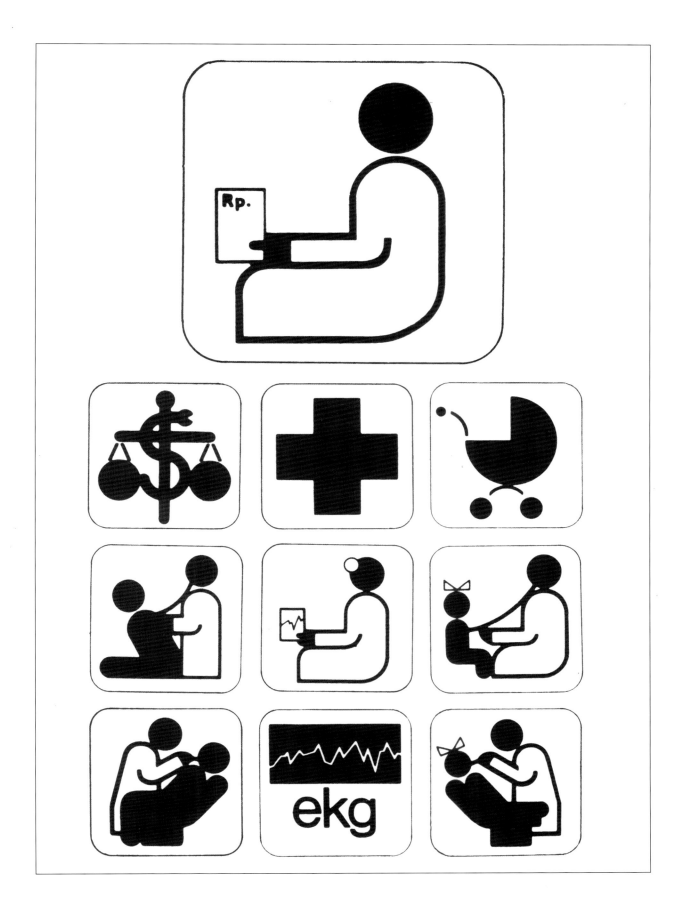

船橋市公園協会
FUNABASHI PARK

「トゥリーくん」

財団法人船橋市公園協会は、船橋市域における緑化の推進及び環境の整備を行うとともに、船橋市の公園、スポーツ・レクリエーション施設の効率的な管理運営と健全な利用の促進を図り、併せて市民の余暇の有効活用を支援し、もってうるおいとやすらぎのある市民生活に寄与することを目的としている。「トゥリーくん」は、船橋市公園協会のために創ったキャラクターで、公園の象徴である樹木をモチーフにデザインした。ロゴマークは、判読性、明晰性、印象に残るようなインパクトの強さに注意して制作した。

「トゥリーくん」

ふなばしアンデルセン公園通年ポスター（1080x728mm）

船橋市公園協会・公園管理センター・清掃車・作業帽

上4点：船橋市公園協会・アンデルセン公園・イベントポスター（364×515mm）

船橋市公園協会・キャラクターコンセプトブック

船橋市公園協会・カタログ合本

船橋市公園協会　2003年カレンダー

船橋市公園協会　2004年カレンダー

船橋市公園協会　2005年カレンダー

ふなばし 三番瀬海浜公園

「アサリくん」

FUNABASHI BAY PARK

「アサリくん」

京葉臨海地域における社会環境の向上を図ることを目的とした三番瀬海浜公園のシンボルキャラクター「アサリくん」は、船橋の海辺に生息し、日常の中で親しまれている生物の代表的なアサリをモチーフとした。ロゴマークは、船橋市公園協会と統一されたデザインで、一貫性を持たせた。

「アサリくん」

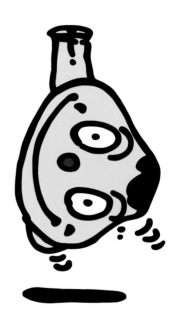

三番瀬海浜公園・海の風景

三番瀬海浜公園・プール

三番瀬海浜公園・エントランス

上5点：三番瀬海浜公園・イベントポスター（364×515mm）

三番瀬海浜公園・パンフレット

三番瀬海浜公園・「アサリくん」グッズ

Takashi Akiyama (Japan)

「トッピー」

クライアントである東武動物公園（東武鉄道）のシンボルキャラクター「トッピー」のデザインの依頼を受けた。要望としては、東武動物公園にデビューする水上木製コースター「レジーナ」にともない、新キャラクターの導入をはかりたいことだった。それで、架空の生き物と地球をイメージしたモチーフを合体させ、地球市民社会のシンボルであるトッピーのキャラクターが誕生した。秋山孝に対する個人指名だったのでとてもやりがいがあり、情熱をかたむけることができた。

「トッピー」

東武動物公園20周年記念ポスター（1080x728mm）

「トッピー」きぐるみ

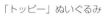
「トッピー」ぬいぐるみ

「トッピー」グッズ

東武動物公園20周年記念・フラッグ

東武動物公園20周年記念・バッジ

「トッピー」ポストカード

「トッピー」像・制作過程

「トッピー」像

1

2

3

4

5

6

just fix it™

7

8

9

1. Metafore 2. EastWest 3. Hungry Hollow 4. Beta Pigs 5. Carl's Jr. 6. Osteogard 7. Perrier 8. Just Fix It 9. Stratford Festival–Juggler Logo

ESTATE planning

AGRI business

1

2

3

jumpstart
GOURMET™

HEALTH & BEAUTY

LIVING
POLICY™

4

5

6

7

8

9

1. The Michael Bossy Group 2. The Michael Bossy Group–AGRIbusiness 3. The Michael Bossy Group–ESTATEplanning 4. Jumpstart Gourmet 5. Spatique 6. Living Policy
7. Inmost Mind–Xseries 8. Inmost Mind–Sound Explorer 9. Inmost Mind–Av Prism

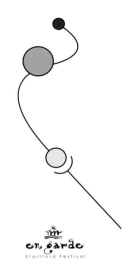

1

2

4

7

8

5

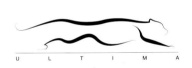

MAXIUM

6

The Discovery Never Ends™

9

10

3

1. Stratford Festival–Miro Logo 2. Dad's Rootbeer 3. Puncher Casual 4. Go North 5. Prototype M 6. Ultima 7. Maxium 8. Maxium Circle 9. Brick Beer 10. Walinga

earcandi

1

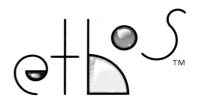

VentureFox

inc

2

ethos™

3

f .stop™

4

marbles
casual fine dining

5

N S M™

network
security
manager

6

JSKH DENTISTRY™

7

DEMEYERE

farms

8

· URBAN LIGHTS ·

9

WOLFHAWK

10

1. Earcandi 2. Venture Fox Inc. 3. Ethos 4. Fstop 5. Marbles 6. Netric 7. JSKS Dentistry 8. Demeyere Farms 9. Urban Lights 10. Wolfhawk

DIL BRANDS

About DIL Brands

Founded in 196 , DIL Brands is a marketing consultancy especialized in brand identity and package design. With offices in Buenos Aires, São Paulo and Santiago, we are associated with DCA Design – for industrial and product design - in Europe and with Coleman BrandWorx – for consumer and retail branding in the USA. We dedicate ourselves to the development of package and product design programs, brand and corporate identity, market research and multimedia services. We invest heavily in high-end computers systems dedicated to graphic and structural design and our offices are connected on-line.

Our Clients are the leading companies in virtually every consumer goods category, including foods, beverages, cosmetics, pharmaceutical products and health and beauty aids. The company is well known for an innovative work method, being the pioneer in the integration of computer and design. Our philosophy has always been oriented to the consumer, what lead us to implement and develop design oriented methodologies for more than 44 years.

We see ourselves as solution providers whose designs - more than being solely attractive - are performance-oriented. Our mission is quite simple: to help our clients sell their products.

We believe that our dedication and success in building long term relationships with our clients is the final proof of the effectiveness of our company's vision and work methodology.

1 Laboratorio Chile
New Brand image
Laboratorio Chile revamped its image as an essential way to bring to the market its mission statement: a solid, expert pharmaceutical company, which manufactures high quality, reliable products, with the lastest technology and accessible to every person..

LABORATORIO CHILE

Before

LABORATORIO**CHILE**®

After

2 SPL
New holding group
A key provider of chemicals in an over
technicized market, SPL needed to express
itself as a global player as well as an
integrated industry. Its new brand image
shows an salt molecule – its fundamental
product – which clearly expresses the
organized complexity of its network
companies.

Before

After

3 Viña Santa Rita
Tradition renewed
A long time leader of the middle range
segment of bottled wines in Chile, 120
renewd the way it sold the legend behind its
name. Type plays a fundamental part here,
expressing modernity out of a font very
contemporary yet familiar.

Before

After

Before

4 General Mills - La Salteña
Homemade
The quintessential expression of an
Argentinian brand, which redesign request
a careful interpretation of the residual
image every consumer would possess of its
message. One of a kind project, when
elements were added other than a brand
scheme simplified.

After

231

Michael Quan - *Managing Director*

81-83 Wigram Street
Parramatta NSW 2150

t +61 2 9891 2888
f +61 2 9891 1283
e designit@triple888.com.au
w www.triple888.com.au

Established 18 years ago, Triple 888 Studios - winner of numerous Australian and International Packaging and Design Awards, is one of Australia's prominent design groups. Our designs have been acclaimed as world class, and displayed in local and international publications.

Home to a team of professional designers who constantly provide creative solutions and services to clients' needs – specialising in every aspect of design from packaging, brochures, corporate identity, promotions, advertisements, marketing materials, web-sites and multi-media, in various languages. We can handle all projects, ranging from small to large.

Our services also include Sales Promotion, Marketing Strategies, Direct Marketing, Event Management, Television and Radio Production, Media Planning, Public Relations and Database Management for specialised clients.

We provide services to local and international clientele and have prepared language specific artwork for Europe, United Kingdom, Asia Pacific, South Africa and Gulf regions.

Our clients consist of manufacturers operating in a wide range of industries including: pharmaceutical, industrial, cosmetics, banking, finance, automotive, housing, homewares and consumables.

1

2

3

4

5

1 1. Parts Peek
2. Truck parts
4. Alberto Estanislao

2 1. IPM Solutions
2. Internet
4. Alberto Estanislao

4 1. Timberland Furniture
2. Furnitures
4. Alberto Estanislao

4 1. Hood Clothing
2. Mens wear
4. Alberto Estanislao

5 1. Premier Fruit & Vegetables
2. Fresh Foods
4. Tamara Chernit

SELECT
Health Products

ORIENT EXPRESS

the,
original
diet

6 1. Select Health
   2. Cosmetics
   3. Health and beauty
   4. Alberto Estanislao

7 1. Sheldon and Hammond
   2. Homewares
   3. Oriental look
   4. Alberto Estanislao

8 1. The Original Diet
   2. Health Foods
   3. Healthy and happy
   4. Alberto Estanislao

1 1. Client Name:
Argos (Mexico)/Telemundo (Miami)
2. Theme of Design:
Corporate Identity for a TV reality show about immigration
of latinoamerican countries to USA.
3. Coments: The mark change depending of the surface;
can to be a grafitti, tatoo, stencil, etc.

2 1. Client Name:
Xpressat (Barcelona)
2. Theme of Design:
Trademark for a telecommunications services company
3. Coments: The mark was inspired in a perforated
computer card. The three orange points represent the
divisions of the company

3 1. Client Name:
Yoochel Kaaj, cinema, video and culture (Mexico)
2. Theme of Design:
Trademark for an audiovisual and cultural association in Yucatan
3. Coments: The name Yoochel Kaaj in mayan lenguage signify
"the look of the people"

234

CONSEJO NACIONAL DE LA FAUNA

4

5

6

4 1. Client Name:
   National Council of the Fauna/Mexico
   2. Theme of Design:
   Corporate Identity of the CNF
   3. Coments:
   The mark represents an animal with referents
   in the aztec culture and a typographical syntesis

5 1. Client Name:
   Editorial Padmapani (Mexico)
   2. Theme of Design:
   Trademark for an editorial of hinduism philosophies
   3. Coments:
   The mark is inspired in the hindu calligraphy

6 1. Client Name:
   The Pearls of the Virgin (Mexico)
   2. Theme of Design:
   Logo for a multimedia and broadcast design studio
   3. Coments:
   The trademark is inspired in a mexican barroque icons

Eric Olivares (Mexico/Spain)

13

14

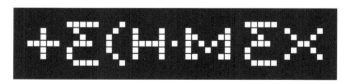

13 1 Client Name:
Atrás de la Raya (Mexico)
2 Theme of Design:
Corporate Identity for a event marketing & promotions agency
3 Coments: The translation of "atrás de la raya" is "beyond the line",
the line and colors change in the diferent aplications

14 1. Client Name:
Tech-Mex (Mexico)
2. Theme of Design:
Trademark for a mexican newmedia art collective
3. Coments: The logo was created with the idea of show folklore,
code, low-tech and high-tech

15

16

17

15   1. Client Name:
Sabia(Mexico)
2. Theme of Design:
Trademark for an agency of entrepreneur capacitation

16   1. Client Name:
Eje Siete (Mexico)
2. Theme of Design:
Trademark of a cultural association

17   1. Client Name:
Moluanda S.L. (Barcelona)
2. Theme of Design:
Logo for an audiovisual production studio

7

8

9

7 1. Client Name:
Camino Real Hotels (Mexico)
2. Theme of Design:
Trademark for the Senda Real Inn hotels
3. Coments: The translation of Senda Real is "Royal Lane"

8 1. Client Name:
Espai d'Art Contemporani de Castelló (Valencia)
2. Theme of Design:
Trademark for a video art proyect and exhibition
3. Coments: The logo continuously is in movement form
and change the central color (blue, green and red)

9 1. Client Name:
Chiquibit (Mexico)
2. Theme of Design:
Trademark for a agency of educational and digital
children meddling
3. Coments: The translation of Chiqui-bit is "Little bit"

10

11

12

10 1. Client Name:
    Tulipandra (Mexico/Netherlands)
    2. Theme of Design:
    Trademark for an agency of business assessment
    and administration
    3. Coments:
    The mark represents a tulip and the letter "t"

11 1. Client Name:
    La Parellada (Barcelona)
    2. Theme of Design:
    Trademark for a mediterranean restaurant

12 1. Client Name:
    Artistic collective (México)
    2. Theme of Design:
    Logo for a interactive videoinstallation project
    "Universal Subway"

1.

1. 1. Discovery Channel
   2. Pilot television show featuring
      refurbishing of classic automobiles

2. 1. Viking Construction
   2. Contractor with scandinavian roots

3. 1. James Brown
   2. Graphic for a line of concert T-Shirts

2.

3.

1.

1. Radiance Medspa Franchise Group
2. Identity for the leader in the medical spa franchise industry

2.

1. Marcel Cosmeceuticals
2. Identity for a line of beauty products

3.

1. Why Weight? Inc.
2. Identity for a womens' 30 minute excercise franchise

1.

radiance™
medspa franchise group

2.

MARCEl
COSMECEUTICALS
FRANCE

3.

Why Weight?

1. 1. Norwegian Cruise Line
    2. Proposed identity for a leading
       cruise vacation company

2. 1. Tor Flyfishing
    2. Identity for a line of flyfishing reels
       based in Norway

3. 1. Sandnes Motoryachts
    2. Identity for a manufacturer of
       luxury yachts in Norway

1.

NORWEGIAN

CRUISE LINE

2.

SANDNES

NORWAY

3.

1.
1. International Union of Architects
2. Proposed identity for the UIA 2005
   conference in Istanbul, Turkey

2.
1. Metaliq Inc.
2. Logo for a James Bond themed client event
   at Metaliq, a Flash developer in San Francisco

3.
1. Sedona Medical Supply
2. Identity for a distributor of Spa related
   equipment and supplies

1.

2.

3.

1.
1. Bungie Software
2. Identity for Halo, a first person shooter
for the X-Box, PC, and Mac

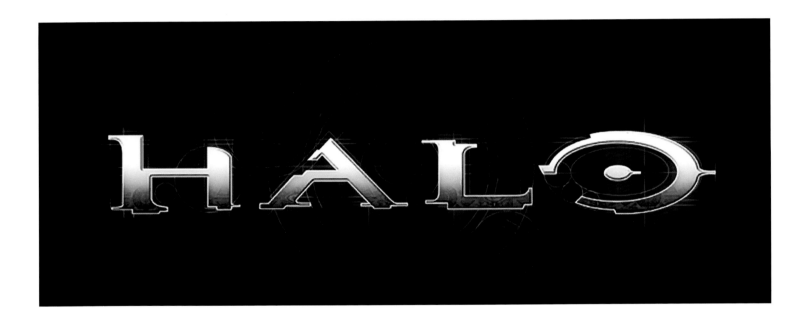

1.

2.

3.

4.

Good Vibes!
Promotions

5.

6.

7.

8.

MOVIE TONE
FILM
A 20TH CENTURY FOX COMPANY

9.

1

2

4

1   1. Client Name: GRADIENT Co.
2. Theme of Design: Patches
3. Comments: Design of logotype and package series for a
new category of cosmetic products - patches - Russia

3   1. Client Name: KIEVMEDPREPARAT
2. Theme of Design: Corporate logo
3. Comments: Due to rebranding, design of corporate
identity for a leading pharmaceutical producer in Ukraine

2   1. Client Name: OLIMP Co.
2. Theme of Design: Cigarettes
3. Comments: Design of logotype and package
series for classic&light cigarrettes

4   1. Client Name: NATURAL TOBACCO Co.
2. Theme of Design: Premium cigarettes
3. Comments: Design of logotype and packaging
for premium class natural tobacco cigarettes

3

5

6

7

MARKETINGMIX

7a

5   1. Client Name: OLIMP Co.
    2. Theme of Design: Juventa ™ Functional beverages
    3. Comments: Design of brand identity for a new category
    of products in Ukraine - functional beverages for youth

7   1. Client Name: Valentine Pertsiya
    2. Theme of Design: Internet journal on marketing
    3. Comments: Redesign of identity

7a 1. Client Name: Valentine Pertsiya
    2. Theme of Design: Internet journal on marketing
    3. Comments: Experimental version of the logotype

6   1. Client Name: ALEPH VINAL Co.
    2. Theme of Design: Wine brand
    3. Comments: Design of logotype for
    a wine brand

8   1. Client Name: OLIMP Co.
    2. Theme of Design: Marseilles ™ Cognac
    3. Comments: Design of brand identity for a
    new mild middle-priced V.S.O.P. cognac

8

1 1. Fondazione Colombo
   2. Logo
   3. Cultural foundation for arts

2 1. Teatro della Gioventù
   2. Logo
   3. Theatre

3 1. Von Pauer
   2. Logo
   3. Polifunctional Medical Centre

4 1. Teatro delle Clarisse
   2. Logo
   3. Theatre

FONDAZIONE
REGIONALE
CRISTOFORO
COLOMBO

1

2

3

4

ORCHIDEE SOMMARIVA

5

ORLANDO
ARREDAMENTO

6

Villa Carmen
Varazze

7

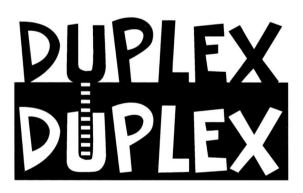

DUPLEX
DUPLEX

8

GARAGE

9

mypersonal**shopper**

XYKHROME
TECHNOLOGIES

DiVINE
ROAD TOURS

windfall
ecology
centre

ZEBRAWARE

EIQ
consultants to creative minds

MAURICE
MASSE
MARKETING

inter*strata*
go beyond.

fitBride

fit personal training

fitBirth

goes the distance

SUMMIT
NATURAL ENERGY BAR

HEADSUP
TALENT AGENCY

conceptegal™
helping to bring life to life.

ostegro™
every day more graceful.

core*reactive*
from vision to fruition

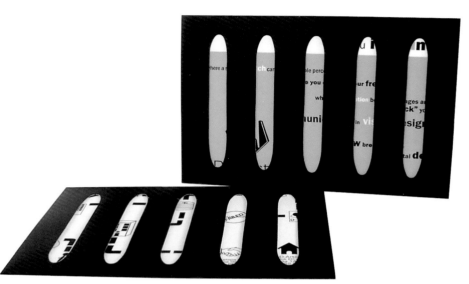

PT. Sentra Duta Nusantara

PT. PARIKESIT KARYA PERWIRA

General Trading - Contractor - Supplier

wahyuhidayat.com

a will to make you better

BODY REPAIR AND MAINTENANCE

1

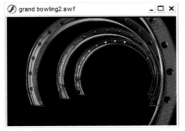

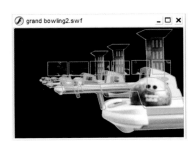

] 1 Company / Studio name: DEZIGNER WEB & GRAPHICS
2 Country: BRAZIL
3 Image number: 01 logotype / 02 poster/ 03 paper and envelope
4 Designer: Daniela Baunsgaard
5 Client: RPPN Paraná
6 Category: ONG
7 Production Date: 2003
8 Theme: Logotype representing the Brasilian Araucária Florest

1

2

3

2 1 Company / Studio name: DEZIGNER WEB & GRAPHICS
2 Country: BRAZIL
3 Image number: 01 logotype / 02 paper and envelope / 03 web site
4 Designer: Daniela Baunsgaard
5 Client: Marketing Business Promoções
6 Category: Strategic Marketing
7 Production Date: 2003
8 Theme: Logotype representing the 4 elements of the Nature:
Water, Air, Fire and Earth.

2

1

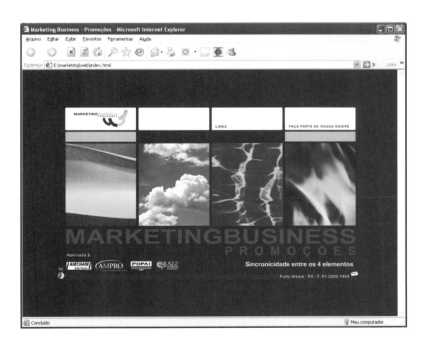

3

DEZIGNER WEB & GRAPHICS (Brazil)

3 1 Company / Studio name: DEZIGNER WEB & GRAPHICS
2 Country: BRAZIL
3 Image number: 01 logotype / 02 web site / 03 banners
4 Designer: Daniela Baunsgaard
5 Client: EC Passage System
6 Category: Sky and Snowboard Insurance
7 Production Date: 2004
8 Theme: Logotype circular representing the transponder inside the snowboard

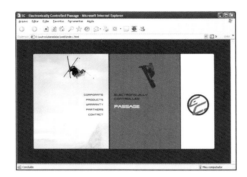

2

1

3

4 1 Company / Studio name: DEZIGNER WEB & GRAPHICS
2 Country: BRAZIL
3 Image number: 01 logotype / 02 visit card / 03 shopping bags
4 Designer: Daniela Baunsgaard
5 Client: Quincy Store
6 Category: Clothing Store
7 Production Date: 2003
8 Theme: Logotype with a green cube representing the letter "Q"

1

2

3

5 1 Company / Studio name: DEZIGNER WEB & GRAPHICS
   2 Country: BRAZIL
   3 Image number: 01 logotype / 02 visit card / 03 paper and envelopes
   4 Designer: Daniela Baunsgaard
   5 Client: Preservação
   6 Category: ONG
   7 Production Date: 2004
   8 Theme: Preservação is an ONG of Brasilian Florest Conservation

1

2

3

1

6 1 Company / Studio name: DEZIGNER WEB & GRAPHICS
2 Country: BRAZIL
3 Image number: 01 logotype / 02 visit card
4 Designer: Daniela Baunsgaard
5 Client: MM Home and Garden
6 Category: Garden and Interior Design
7 Production Date: 2004
8 Theme: Logotype representing the garden and the house in harmony

7 1 Company / Studio name: DEZIGNER WEB & GRAPHICS
2 Country: BRAZIL
3 Image number: 01 logotype / 02 visit card - paper and envelope
4 Designer: Daniela Baunsgaard
5 Client: Focus Consultoria
6 Category: Business Consulting
7 Production Date: 2002
8 Theme: Logotype based on the letter "F" with an eye

Maria Ines Borelli
miborelli@itelefonica.com.br

fone: 11 4033 6987
cel: 11 9836 4137

Alameda Sam Marino, 144
JD. Europa - Bragança Paulista
SP - CEP 12919-500

2

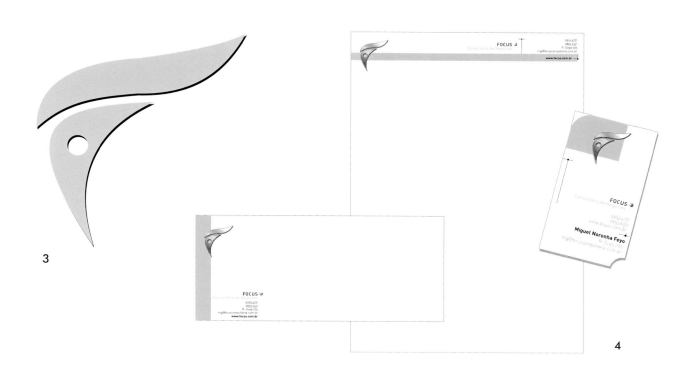

3

4

Icarus Design (India)

Kanan Devan Tea

One of the largest selling brand of Tea in South India, Kanan Devan wished to better align itself with consumer's tastes. Research established that while Kanan Devan consumers appreciated it's unique refreshing taste, a sizable population preferred stronger tea. It was decided that Kanan Devan would bring out a stronger variant as well as different formats - dust and leaf to satisfy varying demands.

Kanan Devan's realignment with consumers was taken a step forward by recreating the brand face. A more approachable typeface combined with a visualization of it's unique origin from the highest mountain range in South India clarified and made it's identity memorable. It's picture-perfect yet "watery English tea" look was transformed into a more robust, refreshing experience. The strong variant was differentiated through a colour change to red and visualization that enhanced strength perceptions.

Kanan Devan Tea

1

1 1. Client Name: Tata Tea
   2. Theme of Design: Origin from some of the
      highest tea gardens in the world.
   3. Comments: Primary variant

2 1. Client Name: Tata Tea
   2. Theme of Design: Origin from some of the
      highest tea gardens in the world.
   3. Comments: Leaf variant

3 1. Client Name: Tata Tea
   2. Theme of Design: Origin from some of the
      highest tea gardens in the world.
   3. Comments: Strong variant

2

3

Fukuda Takehiro (Japan)

Hanegi Toyo Mansion 103 Hanegi Setagaya-ku ,Tokyo 156-0042 Japan

Tel 03-3323-8419

e.mail tovio@ja2.so-net.ne.jp

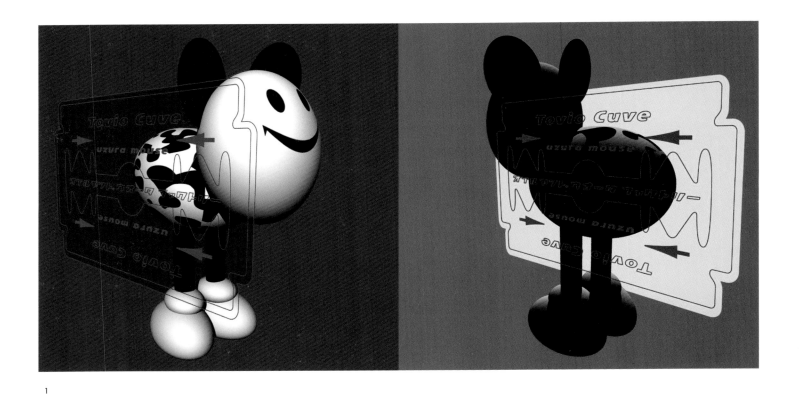

1

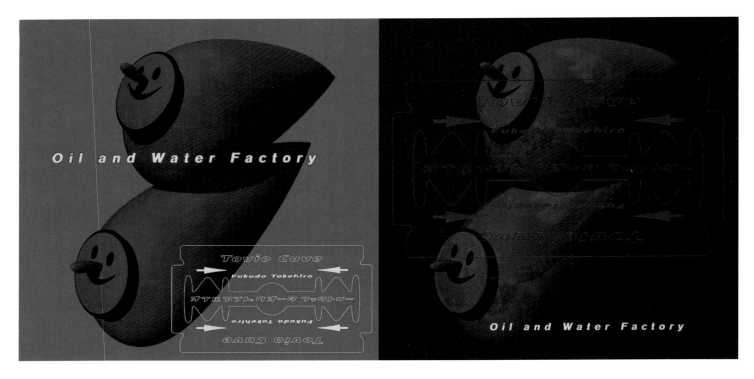

2

1   1.Client Name:Individual work   2   1.Client Name:Individual work
     2.Design,Illustration: Fukuda Takehiro   2.Design,Illustration: Fukuda Takehiro

Chiba Institute of Technology

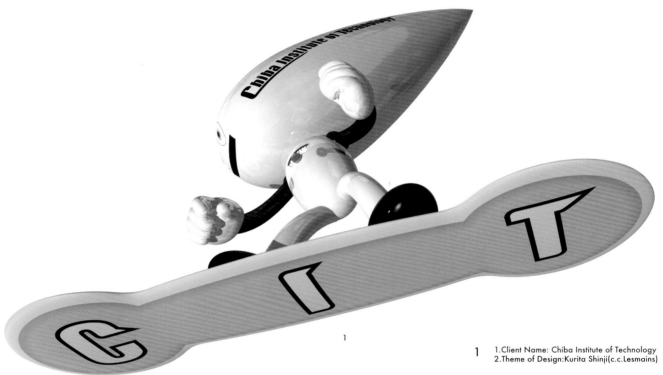

1

1 1.Client Name: Chiba Institute of Technology
2.Theme of Design:Kurita Shinji(c.c.Lesmains)

2 1.Client Name: Victor entertainment
2.Theme of Design: Suzuki Naoyuki(Tycoon Graphics)

2

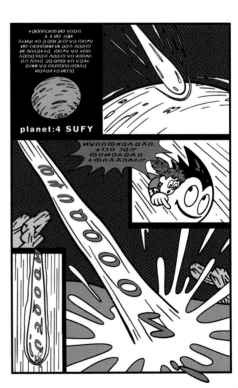

Fukuda Takehiro (Japan)

1

2

3

1   1.Client Name:Individual work
2.Design,Illustration: Fukuda Takehiro

2   1.Client Name:Individual work
2.Design,Illustration: Fukuda Takehiro

3   1.Client Name:Individual work
2.Design,Illustration: Fukuda Takehiro

1   1.Client Name: Matsumoto Kiyoshi
    2.Theme of Design:Fukuda Takehiro+Adex

2   1.Client Name: Shinyusha
    2.Theme of Design:Fukuda Takehiro+Takahashi Koichi

3   1.Client Name: Sony Music Communications
    2.Theme of Design:Yamazaki Hideki(Stove)

RIGHT BRAIN BRANDING (USA)

At Right Brain Branding Consultants, we have worked very hard to become one of the best in strategic design and brand development. Our company is firmly built upon fresh and creative thinking, strong design concepts and the ability to listen and respond rapidly to clients' needs.

Over the past ten years, we have developed an expertise in helping companies improve their image, differentiate their products and services to gain a leading edge in the marketplace through our effective brand management solutions and powerful design concepts, and build equity and value into their most valuable asset — their Brand.

Passion drives us - we don't make management decisions for companies, but we help them to clear the clutter of information by developing strong and powerful Brands, such as the following examples.

1

2

TURBANA

The world's fourth largest banana distributor, Turbana wanted to create an educational tie-in for the nutritional benefits of bananas. We created the "Turbana Twins" that have played a starring role in Turbana's brand transformation and have become a favorite to kids in target geographic regions. Promotional materials and tie-ins have featured the twins and created a buzz on their website which went from hundreds of hits to reach over 250,000 during the launch quarter. An entire new fun and educational website was created, www.TurbanaLand.com

3

FLY ON THE WALL

We developed the Fly On The Wall image, logo and web design from it's inception as a concept being a cutting-edge restaurant review. With the creation and use of an instantly identifiable and striking logo, we were able to define the client's brand and reflect the unique style of reviewing.

4

ADP TOTALSOURCE

A partner with Right Brain for over 8 years, the ADP TotalSource brand was repositioned to focus more on white collar professions. The award winning look branded them as the leader in the market, giving them far greater market share. They now command one of the most profitable departments under the ADP name.

1   Turbana
TurbanaLand Site Entrance
Interactive opening to welcome participants into this fun and educational site.

2   Turbana
Festival Promotions
Life size VW Beetle and characters in costume

5

3   Fly on the Wall
HTML email that gives a "taste" of the newest restaurant reviews.

4   Fly on the Wall
Website Opening
A light and interactive opening for a restaurant review site that is anything but "light"!

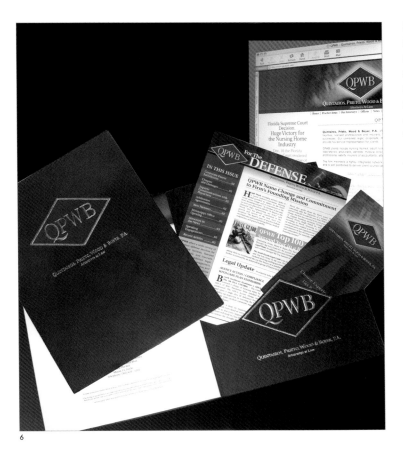

QPWB

QPWB was an existing brand that needed an update to represent it as the new leader in their specialized legal field. We created an exciting and powerful visual presence through the use of color and design, challenging the constraints of stringent bar requirements for this established US law firm.

The result is a much stronger brand that translates across all their materials and reaffirms their strength in their field.

5   ADP TotalSource
Branded materials for sales and marketing. Color coding and design help to organize the numerous brochures needed to present the many services provided.

6   Quinteros, Prieto, Wood & Boyer
Marketing Materials
Textured paper, diecuts and foil embossing add to the powerful visual presence of this growing law firm.

6

269

Clients may get in touch with ICO HQ regarding inquiries to the featured designers in this publication. We can help eliminate the language barrier when dealing with international designers.

e : < icohq@info.email.ne.jp >

■Branding掲載作家へお問い合せご希望の方は、下記 ICO HQへemailをお送り下さい
■ご要望のクリエイターへあなたのご意向をお伝えするコミュニケーション・サポートを行います
■また、このサポートシステムは、掲載作家以外でも、相手の方にご意向をお伝えする事ができます

e : < icohq@info.email.ne.jp >

Company	page	address
Joao Machado Design Lta.	10-13	Rua Padre Xavier Coutinho, 125 4150-751, **Portugal**
Lippincott Mercer	30-35	499 Park Ave. New York, NY 10022, **United States**
Lumen Srl.	94-99	Via Tortona, 4 - 20144 Milan, **Italy**
Maarten Rijnen Illustratie & Design	106-113	Ra 42 1276 HT Huizen, **Netherlands**
Marta Rourich Deseno Grafico	44-47	Putxet 80-82 1°A, 08023 Barcelona, **Spain**
Mike Quon Designation Inc.	114-121	543 River Road, Fair Haven, New Jersey 07704, **United States**
Minale Tattersfield & Partners	74-79	The Poppy Factory, 20 Petersham Road, Richmond, Surrey TW10 6UR, **United Kingdom**
Montobbiodesign	248-249	Via Caffa 5/4 Genova, **Italy**
Mountain Design BV	204-207	Paleisstraat 6, 2514 JA The Hague, **Netherlands**
Pisarkiewicz Mazur & Co. Inc.	132 - 137	307 West 38th Street New York, NY 10018, **United States**
Proad Image Design	210 - 217	3rd Floor, No. 224 Teh Sing East Road, Taipei, **Taiwan, R.O.C.**
Right Brain Branding Consultants	268 - 269	10931 SW 161 Place, Miami, Florida 33196, **United States**
Russell Leong Design	36-43	847 Emerson Street Palo Alto, California 94301, **United States**
Scribblers' Club	226-229	969 Guelph Street, Kitchener, Ontario, **Canada**
Solutions	156-161	Sternstrasse 117, 20357 Hamburg, **Germany**
Stang	48-55	Heemraadssingel 86, 3021 De Rotterdam, **Netherlands**
Stony Image	176-181	Tower C, 8F, No. 96, sec. 1, HSIN-TAI 5th, Rd., HIS--CHIH, Taipei Hsien, **Taiwan**
Studioa	100-105	Avenida Salaverry 3328 Lima 17, **Peru**
SUPER STUDIO ,INC.	138-141	1-5-13-7F Jinnan, Shibuya-ku,Tokyo 151-0041, **Japan**
Team Creatif	196-197	89, rue de Miromesnil 75008 Paris, **France**
the Lemon Yellow	142-145	9F-3, No. 512. sec. 4, Chung-Hsiao E, Rd. Taipei, **Taiwan**
Tor Naerheim Brand Design	240-245	30699 Russell Ranch Road, Suite 190 Westlake Village, CA 91362, **United States**
Tridimage	26-29	Av. Cramer 1718 9C, C1426APD, Buenos Aires, **Argentina**
Triple888 Studio	232-233	81-83 Wigram Street Parramatta NSW 2150, **Australia**
Tucker Creative Pty Ltd.	80-85	105/117 North Road, Nairne South Australia 5252, **Australia**
Tucker Design	150-155	The Church Hall 6a George Street, Stepney South Australia 5069, **Australia**
Zero Design Ltd.	208-209	The Coach House, Northumberland Street South East Lane, Edinburgh EH3 6LP,**Scotland**

ICO HQ. *International Creators' Organization / Headquarters*   13-14, Wakamatsu-Cho, Chigasaki, Kanagawa JAPAN post 253-0051   e : < icohq@info.email.ne.jp >

EPILOGUE

Finally we have compiled our new Branding book title and launched it from the ICO Port towards new markets worldwide. We hope these featured designers, art directors and artists will expand their business possibilities more and more internationally.I would like to acknowledge and give my deepest appreciation to the following people who have given us so much of their tireless support and critical contributions for this publication of Branding :

Jacques Evrard, Jo Sickbert, Colette Cotte, Eddie Archer, Yashi Okita, Koichi Yangaizawa, Ute Von Buch, Gerard Caron, Marta Rourich Esq.

Thanks and warm regards,

ICO HQ.
Norio Mochizuki

Title / BRANDING LOGO & MARK
Released / Sep. 2005
Art Supervision / Yumiko Mochizuki, Robert Morris, Satoru Shiraishi,
Cover Design / Norio Mochizuki
Editorial Design & Layout / Yumiko Mochizuki
Editorial Staff / Satoru Shiraishi, Kazuhito Mochizuki, Xuanji Wang, Robert Morris,
Front Cover Images / Stang Gubbels
Translation / Robert Morris, Jo Sickbert,
Prologue / Robert Morris,
■Publishing House / ICO CO., LTD.
ICO (International Creators' Organization)
Post Code 253-0051 13-14 Wakamatsu-cho, Chigasaki, Kanagawa, JAPAN
url : http://www.1worldart.com/
e : ico-nori@info.email.ne.jp   f : 81- (0)467-86-8944   u : http://www.1worldart.com/
Copyright : ©International Creators' Organization (ICO)

Distributor : AZUR /Beijing DesignerBooks Co., Ltd.
Publisher / Norio Mochizuki

■ ICO Publication Project :
  ICO HQ. Norio Mochizuki / ico-nori@info.email.ne.jp
  ICO AMERICA Robert Morris / icoamerica@cox.net
  ICO JAPAN Satoru Shiraishi / c-wave@gaea.ocn.ne.jp
  ICO CHINA Chen Zhong / ctibooks@x263.net

タイトル / BRANDING LOGO & MARK
発行日 / 2005年9月
編集制作 / 望月 由美子、ロバート・モーリス、白石 智、望月 かずひと、王萱佶
表紙デザイン / 望月 紀男
表紙カバーイラスト : □ Stang Gubbels
本文レイアウト・デザイン構成 / 望月 由美子
翻訳 / □ Robert Morris □ Jo Sickbert
発行所 / ICO CO., LTD. Publishing House ICO (International Creators' Organization)
〒253-0051 神奈川県茅ヶ崎市若松町13-14

定価：9,450 Yen (本体/9,000円＋税)   ISBN 4-931154-17-4 C3272